one-to-one

one-to-one

the effective way to nurture Christians

Stephen Gaukroger
and David Warren
with Simon Fox

CROSSWAY BOOKS
38 De Montfort Street, Leicester LE1 7GP, England

© 1997, Stephen Gaukroger and David Warren

First published 1997

British Library Cataloguing in Publication Data
A catalogue record for this book is available from the British
Library.

ISBN 1–85684–153–7

Set in Garamond No. 3 and Bauer Bodoni

Typeset in Great Britain by Parker Typesetting Service,
Leicester

Printed in Great Britain

contents

Preface

How many of us have enjoyed the privilege and sheer relief of having someone else's undivided attention? And if we know that that person's concern is to help us where we most need help, in the development of our Christian faith and its application to our problems of ignorance, confusion, doubt, fear or inadequacy, how much more would we value such attention?

Of course, if you can afford it you can buy the attention of a psychiatrist or professional counsellor (and what a great job many of them do). But how much better it would be to find mutual help within your church fellowship, developing a shared faith between a discipler and disciple. This kind of sharing goes much further than answering our inward cry for attention; it establishes our faith and encourages a new hunger for growth, action and fellowship.

If you think this is an idealized description of one-to-one discipling, rest assured that it can happen. It is a wonderfully encouraging experience and it need not be limited to the few weeks after a new Christian has come to faith. Older people need to be discipled too. So do ministers. If you are quite well on in years and in

Christian experience would you not value a six-week's course with another Christian, say a couple of hours a week?

This approach with all its benefits for the discipler as well as the disciple is well within the range of all churches – even the tiniest fellowship can surely find one or two people who can help one another. It costs nothing except time in preparation and in meeting and the rewards are uncountable.

This book sets out the basic principles behind the concept of one-to-one discipling in simple, straightforward terms. It is for churches and individuals to interpret the principles in practice in ways which will suit them best. A cut and dried syllabus which suits situation A would be of no use in situation B, so we have not attempted to burden the reader with detailed programmes. Do, however, look at pages 157–159 for further help. We have also suggested a few practical ideas at the end of each of the five sections of the book.

Remember too that some people might prefer to run a marathon rather than sit down with one other person to talk about their faith! Some people learn better in groups and are embarrassed by individual closeness. We need to be sensitive to their needs and not bully them.

Having said this, it may well be that a carefully monitored, well-organized scheme of one-to-one discipling, supported by prayer, might bring about a quiet revolution in your church. How about it?

1

What is discipling?

chapter one

Biblical principles
A follower

What is a disciple? First, the New Testament describes
the disciple as a *follower* of Jesus Christ. As Jesus was
walking beside the Sea of Galilee he met the fishermen
Simon and Andrew. Jesus said to them, 'Come, follow
me, and I will make you fishers of men.' We read that 'At
once they left their nets and followed him.' After that
Jesus met two other fishermen, James and John, and
called them to follow him too (Matthew 4:18–22).

The gospels make it clear that following Jesus not
only meant accompanying him, but also being willing to
relinquish anything and everything that was inconsistent
with being his disciple. In some cases this meant giving
up their jobs, as in the case of the four fishermen in
Matthew 4:20–22, and Levi the tax collector in Luke
5:28; in other cases it meant giving up their possessions,
as in the case of the rich young man in Matthew 19, who
decided that the cost of being Jesus' disciple was too
high.

To follow Jesus was to be involved in the same
ministry as he was, to proclaim the same message and to

do the same mighty works as he was doing, in his name and with his authority (see Mark 3:13–19). Following Jesus also meant adopting his attitude of self-denial and even being ready to die for his sake (see Mark 8:34–38).

Jesus called his followers to an unconditional discipling in which they were to 'follow in his steps' (1 Peter 2:21), doing the things he did. The '144,000' who are mentioned in the book of Revelation are those who 'follow the Lamb wherever he goes' (Revelation 14:4). They are the 'called, chosen and faithful followers' of Jesus (Revelation 17:14), those who have been called and chosen by him and who have been faithful to him by their own personal resolve, which has been made possible by Jesus' faithfulness to them.

A learner

Secondly, the New Testament portrays the disciple as a *learner* – someone who learns from Jesus, who is his pupil, student or apprentice, who hears, understands and obeys the words of the Teacher and Master. The followers of Moses, John the Baptist and the Pharisees are all referred to by the New Testament as pupils learning from their teacher (see John 9:28; 1:35; Mark 2:18). Jesus too called his disciples to learn from him: 'Take my yoke upon you and learn from me' (Matthew 11:29).

They were to learn from him 'on the job', while serving him. They were involved in a constant learning process. Their attempts to serve him often revealed their lack of understanding. For example, when people brought their children to Jesus so that he could bless them, the disciples (presumably thinking that Jesus didn't want to be bothered with little children) tried to discourage the parents from doing this. But Jesus rebuked the disciples, saying, 'Let the little children come to me, and do not hinder them, for the kingdom of God belongs to such as these' (Mark 10:13–16).

The disciples of Jesus were called 'learners' long before they were called 'Christians' – in fact, that name was first used only after Jesus' ascension to heaven (see Acts 11:26). The New Testament shows us that we cannot be disciples of Jesus without also being his learners: we cannot follow him without learning from him.

An imitator

Thirdly, the New Testament shows us that the disciple should be an *imitator* of Jesus, someone who models his or her behaviour on the example of Jesus. This strand of discipling is emphasized mostly in Paul's letters, but also in John's letters and the Letter to the Hebrews (see Hebrews 6:12; 13:7; 3 John 11). These New Testament passages encourage us to model ourselves on God (Ephesians 5:1; 1 Thessalonians 1:6) and on human teachers (Philippians 3:17; 2 Thessalonians 3:7, 9), who themselves are imitating God (1 Corinthians 11:1) and are part of churches which deserve to be imitated (1 Thessalonians 2:14).

The New Testament also challenges us to look to our own character and way of life to see what there is about us that is worthy of imitation by others. Sometimes Christians who are younger in the faith than we are, and whom we are discipling, may imitate not only the important aspects of our behaviour which we want them to copy, but also the more marginal aspects which don't really matter, and even the negative things which we try to hide! The disciple should imitate 'faith' (Hebrews 13:7), 'patience' (Hebrews 6:12) and 'good' (3 John 11) in the discipler's behaviour and character.

Making a journey

So we have seen that a *disciple* is a follower of Jesus Christ, and that a *discipler* is a disciple who wants to help other disciples to follow Jesus. *Discipling* is the process in which disciples and disciplers come together so that the disciples can receive help to follow Jesus. *One-to-one discipling*, the subject of this book, is a particular method of discipling involving one disciple and one discipler. The Bible provides us with a number of illuminating pictures of this kind of discipling.

In one of these biblical pictures the disciple is portrayed as *making a journey*. Christ is the fellow traveller who always accompanies us, even when we fail to recognize his presence (see Luke 24:15–16).

While Jesus walks with us, we are also meant to walk with other Christians and especially to try to walk in their shoes. In some cases we will walk beside another disciple throughout our lives (for example, our marriage partner, Christian siblings or lifelong Christian friends), while in other cases we will be walking together for just a small part of the journey. Disciples must be willing to walk at the same speed and in the same direction as their fellow travellers, while being willing, if asked, to set the pace or alter the direction. Sometimes there will be a need to carry a load for other travellers or to support them or even carry them. Sometimes there will be animated conversation along the journey, but at other times there will be silence. Sometimes travellers will have common interests, while at other times they will have differing ones. Ultimately it is being there on the journey with the other travellers which is more important than what we say or do.

Telling a story

This is another biblical picture of discipling. For disciplers to help disciples to grow spiritually, they need to hear the story of their disciple's life. Disciples must always have the freedom to tell their story in their own way. It should be accepted as given, with the discipler only asking for clarification, not correcting or challenging. The story may be retold often, the *differences* in the telling being clues to the changing moods and perspectives of the disciple, and the *constants* showing which are the most important parts of the story. Once the story has been fully told, the discipler must tell it back to the disciple so that the disciple knows that it has been fully comprehended. Only then can the discipler begin to explore with the disciple what the story says; only then can true discussion begin.

A memorable New Testament example of this process is the conversation which the risen Jesus had with the two disciples on the road to Emmaus (see Luke 24:13–35). Jesus, the Teacher or discipler, 'came up and walked along with them; but they were kept from recognising him. He asked them, "What are you discussing as you walk along?"' Jesus was asking them to tell him their personal story. They then told him all about himself – his ministry, his crucifixion, the empty tomb, the angels . . . Having listened to their story, Jesus patiently showed them what it all meant: 'beginning with Moses and all the Prophets, he explained to them what was said in all the Scriptures concerning himself.'

Tending a plant

This is a biblical picture both of the relationship between the disciple and God and the relationship between a disciple and a caring discipler. God is the gardener who will not break the bruised reed (Isaiah 42:3; Matthew 12:20), but will dig and prune (John 15:1–2) in order to bring about growth and a good crop. The discipler should also be a gardener. Paul describes disciplers as 'fellow-workers' in 'God's field', who work to make the disciples who have been 'planted' grow (1 Corinthians 3:6–9). Disciplers must carry out their part of this process with diligence, care and concern. The plant must be encouraged to grow in the right soil and conditions, and it must also be directed in that growth by training and shaping.

The discipler should remember that the ultimate goal for the plant is not its size or strength or shape but the quantity and quality of the *crop* which it produces. Like Jesus, the discipler must be looking for fruit and will be disappointed when there is none (Matthew 21:18–19). The disciple's ability to bear fruit comes not from the discipler but as a result of the disciple growing in Christ (John 15:4–5).

Restoring a picture

It can be helpful to think of discipling as a process which is similar to restoring a painting. All people are made in the image of God (Genesis 1:26–27), but that image has been defaced by our sin, so the picture needs to be restored. Care is needed so that the fabric is not damaged; only the dirt is removed and not the paint. Any additions which are made must be done in the material and style of the original. The restorer (that is, the discipler) needs to be in tune with the artist (that is, God), knowing what his original design for the picture was and working on it in the same way in which the artist himself first worked. The aim of restorers is not to bring attention to themselves, but to allow the splendour of the artist to shine through. Both discipler and disciple must allow the picture which is revealed to be the character of Christ (Colossians 3:10). Like the 'letter from Christ' which Paul says we are to be (2 Corinthians 3:3), which can only be written by Jesus, the picture can only be restored by the Spirit of the Living God working upon human hearts.

Shepherding a sheep

The Lord who is the shepherd (Psalm 23:1; John 10:11, 14) places his sheep in the care of trusted 'under-shepherds' to be in charge of his people (Jeremiah 3:15; 23:4; Ezekiel 34:23). Both Paul and Peter speak of the 'shepherds of the church of God' and the 'shepherds of God's flock' (Acts 20:28; 1 Peter 5:2). Under-shepherds, or disciplers, are to tend the flock of disciples by feeding, watering, leading, guiding, protecting and healing them. Disciplers need to be filled with the compassion of Christ, who saw people as 'sheep without a shepherd' (Matthew 9:36).

God's solemn warning through the prophet Ezekiel (Ezekiel 34:1–10) is that although he will step in when his shepherds abdicate their duty, he will still hold them accountable for the sheep. So disciplers must not take their task lightly or thoughtlessly and must never deliberately abandon their disciples.

chapter two

Biblical examples

The Bible gives us a number of examples of one-to-one discipling. Both the lessons of the good and the warnings of the bad need to be heeded.

Moses and Joshua

The career of Joshua provides one of the most extensive Old Testament examples of good discipling. The process by which Joshua moves from being Moses' young assistant to Israel's new leader is one in which God uses Moses as the discipler. We can see six steps in Moses' discipling of Joshua.

1. Moses recognized Joshua's personality, abilities and gifts

Moses and Joshua had very different personalities and abilities. For example, Joshua fought in the valley while Moses prayed on the mountain (Exodus 17:8–16); Joshua stayed in the tent of meeting while Moses returned to the people in the camp (Exodus 33:11). Understanding and accepting their differences was an important part of the discipling process. Joshua's abilities and gifts were recognized and assessed by Moses so that they could be developed and refined. He remained basically the same man, but new depths and dimensions of his character were uncovered. For example, he remained a fighter, but he also became a man who trusted in God's power (see Joshua 5:13–6:27).

2. Moses taught Joshua by word and example

Joshua accompanied Moses up on to the mountain of God (Exodus 24:13); he was encouraged by Moses to enter the land and to lead Israel to inherit it (Deuteronomy 1:38); he was corrected by Moses (see, for example, Exodus 32:17–18); and he was told by Moses to let the prophets prophesy rather than stop them (Numbers 11:26–29). Moses discipled Joshua not only in words but also by actions. During his years as Moses' assistant Joshua probably learned more from watching Moses than from listening to him. Joshua learned not only from Moses' successes but also from his mistakes; he saw some things which he should copy and others which he should avoid.

3. Moses gave Joshua more and more opportunity and responsibility

The training of a disciple must progress from the stage where the discipler does something and the disciple watches, to where the discipler and the disciple do and watch together, and finally, to where the disciple does and the discipler watches. It is hard to hand over responsibility, but if opportunities to grow are never given, the disciple will never really learn. Moses gave Joshua the task of exploring the land (Numbers 13:16; 14:6) and assigning it to the tribes (Numbers 34:17). When Moses gave Joshua this opportunity and responsibility he, Moses, did not know that he himself was not going to enter the promised land: he did not know that Joshua would lead the people during this crucial phase of their history without his assistance. If Moses had not given Joshua some lesser responsibility in the earlier stages, he would not have been ready to take over as leader when Moses died.

4. Joshua's character developed

Joshua became a man of the Spirit (Numbers 27:18) who wholeheartedly followed the Lord (Numbers 32:12). Over the years which he spent as Moses' pupil, he came to resemble his teacher, a man with whom God had spoken face to face (Numbers 12:6–8; Deuteronomy 34:10–12). Moses had seen the glory of God and his character radiated that glory (Exodus 34:29–35), so when people were in Moses' presence they had to respond to that glory, either accepting or rejecting it. As Joshua spent time with Moses, that glory of God shone on him and, in the words of Paul, he became 'transformed into God's likeness with ever-increasing glory' (2 Corinthians 3:12–18). It was a godliness which was not so much taught as caught.

5. Moses eventually handed over
the leadership to Joshua

Moses had to commission, encourage and strengthen
Joshua so that he could be the next leader of the people
(Deuteronomy 3:28; 31:1–8, 14). It was a bitter pill for
Moses that God did not allow him to enter the promised
land, but that pill was sweetened by the assurance that
God would be faithful and would lead his people on
through Joshua. There was no vindictive power struggle
or messy leadership battle here. Instead, with grace and
dignity, Moses identified Joshua as the new leader and
gave him his total support in the change-over. For Moses
and Joshua this was the natural outcome of the discipling
process which had been going on for many years. Their
first recorded encounter at Rephidim had set in motion a
train of events which inevitably led to this day, and a
process which the Lord himself directed (Exodus 17:8–
16).

6. Joshua was acknowledged as a leader
by God and his people

God said of Joshua, 'As I was with Moses, so I will be
with you' (Joshua 1:5), and the people said to him,
'Just as we fully obeyed Moses, so we will obey you'
(Joshua 1:17). The true test of the effectiveness of
discipling is not so much the assessment of the disciple
or even that of the discipler, but that of God and his
people. The verdict of Scripture is clearly that Joshua
was a leader anointed by God. Joshua is often
mentioned alongside Moses in the rest of the Old

Testament and in the New, for example in Stephen's sermon (Acts 7:44–45), and the faith exploits of both appear in Hebrews 11:24–31. Joshua was remembered with reverence because he had brought real benefit to the people. The book of Joshua ends by saying that 'Israel served the LORD throughout the lifetime of Joshua and of the elders who outlived him and who had experienced everything the LORD had done for Israel' (Joshua 24:31).

David and Solomon

The case of David and Solomon highlights the importance of discipling in training a young and inexperienced person (see 1 Chronicles 22:5). It also reminds us that lessons must be learnt not only once but again and again, for Solomon started well in the ways of David (2 Chronicles 1:1), but at the end of his life rejected those ways (1 Kings 11:4–6). It has been said that God has no grandchildren, so while parents (both physical and spiritual) have a duty to bring up their children 'in the training and instruction of the Lord' (Ephesians 6:4), there must also be a coming of age when the child takes personal responsibility for his or her life and becomes a child of God (or not). Solomon started well by asking God for wisdom and discernment rather than long life, or wealth, or the death of his enemies (1 Kings 3:4–15), but by living only on the legacy of that choice he eventually became bankrupt and then started making wrong choices (1 Kings 11:1–6). It seems that his faith in God never really grew beyond this childlike point of asking for wisdom; he failed to develop a mature, adult commitment to God in which he took full responsibility for his own actions and kept on learning and growing spiritually.

Elijah and Elisha

The two prophets Elijah and Elisha are another example of good discipling. Elisha was called by God to be Elijah's attendant and then his successor as prophet (1 Kings 19:16–21), and this calling was recognized by others, who said, 'The spirit of Elijah is resting on Elisha' (2 Kings 2:15). Elisha knew that in order to follow Elijah he would have to leave behind his family and his work. Elijah's spirit was symbolized by his cloak, and when he was finally taken away from Elisha by God, the disciple still had his teacher's cloak and a double portion of his spirit (2 Kings 2:1–15). This shows us the attitude which a disciple should have towards his discipler: respect and remembrance but not worship or undue dependence.

Eli and his sons

Eli was the priest in charge of the tabernacle at Shiloh, and his family are an outstanding example of bad discipling. Eli had failed to discipline his sons (1 Samuel 3:13), and their behaviour was disgraceful (see 1 Samuel 2:12–17). The disastrous result was the capture of the ark of the covenant by the Philistines (1 Samuel 4:21–22). The fact that Eli seems to have been able to

24

disciple Samuel but not his own sons is a warning to us not to be so involved with others that we neglect those closest to us. It is also an encouragement to us, because it shows that mistakes need not debar us from ever serving God again, for he is the God of second opportunities (1 Samuel 2:11; 3:1). Against all Eli's failures must be set his ability to help the young Samuel to recognize, listen, and speak to the Lord (1 Samuel 3:8–10). The very heart of discipling is to be able to help someone say, 'Speak, LORD, for your servant is listening.'

Solomon and Rehoboam

The case of Solomon and Rehoboam shows us that when the discipling which has been received is rejected by the disciple, then the inevitable result is the termination of the whole discipling process from one generation to another. Solomon, having in later life rejected his father David's ways, failed to point his own son Rehoboam in the right direction, and eventually the kingdom was permanently divided (1 Kings 12:16). Rehoboam had not been discipled by Solomon for kingship, and when he faced his first test, he even rejected the advice of the elders who had served his father, accepting instead the advice of his equally ill-prepared contemporaries, the young men who had grown up with him and served him (1 Kings 12:6–11). This shows us that discipling which is not properly given or fully integrated into a person's life will rarely withstand the competition of seemingly more attractive and palatable advice.

Jesus

The Lord Jesus himself is the supreme example of the true discipler. He invested a great deal of time, energy, patience and love in the lives of his disciples. The public ministry of Jesus was about three years long, and yet the recorded events could all have taken place in the space of about one month. Clearly there were other public events which are not recorded in the gospels (see John 20:30–31; 21:24–25), but the summary sentences about Jesus and his disciples suggest that he gave a great deal of time to them (see Matthew 11:1; Mark 6:1; Luke 8:1). While he would have spent some of this time teaching them as a group, he would also have spent much of it speaking to them on a one-to-one basis.

He discipled by *example*, *word*, *action* and *sending*. They saw in Jesus the perfect pattern of someone who was fully and completely following God. His teaching grounded them in the truth of God so that they could eventually preach and write it for others. The deeds of Jesus built up their faith so that in time they could perform miracles in his name. His sending them, as the Father had sent him, refined and tested their following.

Peter, John and James

In the gospels we see that these three men were discipled by Jesus with particular care. He called them by name to follow him (Mark 1:14–20); he gave them new names (Mark 3:16–17); they were present at significant events such as the healing of the young girl at Jairus' house (Mark 5:37), the Transfiguration (Mark 9:2) and Jesus' arrest at

Gethsemane (Mark 14:33). Jesus discipled Peter individually at the Lake of Gennesaret (Luke 5:1–11), at Caesarea Philippi (Mark 8:27–38) and at the Sea of Tiberias (John 21:15–23); he discipled John in the Upper Room (John 13:23–26) and at Golgotha (John 19:25–27). No wonder these three men became the apostles of Christ and the 'pillars' of the church (Acts 1:13; Galatians 2:9).

Barnabas and Paul

These two men are an interesting New Testament example of discipling. At first it was Barnabas, the 'Son of Encouragement' (Acts 4:36), who discipled Paul and brought him into Christian fellowship (Acts 9:27). He encouraged Paul to mix with other Christians, to exercise his teaching ministry (Acts 11:25–30) and to get involved in·mission (Acts 12:25). Later, however, it was Paul who discipled Barnabas, teaching him about public speaking (Acts 13:42), facing 'dispute and debate' (Acts 15:2, 39), recognizing God's grace (Galatians 2:9), and challenging hypocrisy, which had led him astray (Galatians 2:13). Discipling must always be a two-way process, and often the disciple becomes the discipler. It is a sure sign that the discipler is spiritually mature if he can graciously and willingly let his disciple grow and develop even beyond his own level of maturity.

John Mark

John Mark was at first discipled by both Barnabas and Saul (Acts 12:25), then by Barnabas alone (Acts 15:39), and finally by Paul again (2 Timothy 4:11). He also received some spiritual input from Peter (1 Peter 5:13). When John Mark left Paul and Barnabas midway through the first missionary journey (Acts 13:13), serious repercussions resulted, but Barnabas' costly decision to continue to disciple him (Acts 15:37) in time bore fruit in a renewed John Mark who became both helpful to Paul in his ministry and a son to Peter.

Disciplers must ask God for the faith to see the potential in each disciple, the patience not to be put off by the first disaster, and the wisdom to know when to continue and when to stop. Our prayer for our discipling work should be: 'O Lord, grant me the serenity to accept the things I cannot change; the courage to change the things I can; and the wisdom to know the difference.'

Silas, Timothy and Titus

Paul also had a number of other disciples. After the split with Barnabas and John Mark, he discipled Silas (Acts 15:40), who also seems to have been taught by Peter (1 Peter 5:12). Timothy (Acts 16:1–5) is described as Paul's 'helper' (Acts 19:22), 'fellow-worker' (Romans 16:21) and 'brother' (2 Corinthians 1:1), and as a 'servant of Christ Jesus' (Philippians 1:1) who had 'proved himself . . . in the work of the gospel' (Philippians 2:22). Titus (Galatians 2:1) was a disciple in whom Paul felt he could rightly boast (2 Corinthians 7:13–14).

In the cases of these last two we have some written discipling material – Paul's two letters to Timothy and his one letter to Titus. These letters are the clearest examples of one-to-one discipling in the New Testament. Both Timothy and Titus are described as Paul's sons, and the personal references throughout the letters reveal the close relationship between Paul and each of them. Paul corrects, encourages, rebukes, reminds and warns them (2 Timothy 4:2; Titus 2:15). He is concerned about their spiritual lives and leadership, their mental understanding and development, and their physical needs and situations. All disciplers and disciples could learn a great deal by carefully reading and studying these three books (see Michael Griffiths, *Timothy and Titus: Crossway Bible Guide* (Crossway Books, 1996)).

The shepherd and the sheep

Alongside the examples of discipling in the Bible, there are also some broader images of the discipling process. Three of these are particularly common in both the Old and New Testaments. First, there is the picture of the shepherd and the sheep.

Both Psalm 23 and John 10 speak about the Lord, the good shepherd, discipling his sheep. He directs and protects them, he feeds and heals them, he knows them and is known by them. Peter, no doubt remembering Jesus' teaching and example, describes him as 'the Shepherd and Overseer of your souls' (1 Peter 2:25). He says to Christian leaders, 'Be shepherds of God's flock that is under your care, serving as overseers' under the authority of the 'Chief Shepherd', 'not because you must, but because you are willing, as God wants you to be' (1 Peter 5:2–4). Paul also describes leaders as 'shepherds of the church of God' (Acts 20:28). Jude speaks about 'shepherds who feed only themselves', an echo of Jesus' judgment against the 'hired hand' who 'cares nothing for the sheep' (Jude 12; John 10:12–13).

The potter and the clay

Jeremiah 18:1–6 and Romans 9:21 emphasize God's absolute authority to do and make as he sees fit (see also Isaiah 29:16; 45:9; 64:8). While he is the supreme Potter who kneads and moulds the clay of people's personalities – forming and shaping it, even remaking a marred pot – we are his fellow-workers (1 Corinthians 3:9; 2 Corinthians 6:1) and, under his direction, we work the clay of others' lives to become the pottery which God wants. God can form our own lives while we ourselves are being used by him to form the lives of others. He is no-one's debtor, and what we invest in others brings dividends not only to them but also to us. Some of the hidden flaws and defects in our lives will be revealed and remedied only as we come under the scrutiny of the person we are discipling.

The builder and the stones

1 Peter 2:4–10 echoes the Old Testament theme of God taking individuals and making them into his building. Paul develops the analogy of building in 1 Corinthians 3:9–17, where God, Paul and other Christians are all depicted as builders. Paul warns that each Christian 'should be careful how he builds' (verse 10). He stresses the importance of having the right foundation: 'no-one can lay any foundation other than the one already laid,

which is Jesus Christ' (verse 11). There is a double dimension here, for we are both the building and the builders. As we build others into God's building, so we are built into it ourselves. As we help to shape other stones and to set them in place, it also becomes clear what sort of stones we are ourselves and where we should be placed in the structure of the building. The warning of those who rejected *the* Stone, Jesus Christ, and so stumbled and fell (1 Peter 2:7–8) should guard us against rejecting either Christ or other Christians – the living stones whom he has chosen as precious.

chapter three

Contemporary examples
Conversion discipling

Numerous local, national and even international evange-listic crusades have emphasized the need for conversion discipling. The 'counsellor' at the event and the 'discipler' in follow-up are integral parts of such crusades. Training is given to those who will be involved, and often converts are only referred to churches which are qualified to receive them.

The critical nature of this discipling is well under-stood and studies constantly show how those who are not adequately discipled soon slip away. The church has not fully learned the lessons, but much progress has been made. One-to-one discipling is an important part of this process and can either stand on its own or in conjunction with group discipling.

Conversion discipling should never be seen as an end in itself, but always as the prelude to further discipling for the whole of the Christian life which has just begun. If the church disciples only at the beginning, it will inevitably produce weak and dying converts. Discipling must begin as it intends to go on, with more than just good intentions.

The Christian life

Discipling for the whole of the Christian life is an established part of church life. There are now numerous organizations, courses and structures which offer help in the many aspects of Christian living. These sometimes lack the personal touch and depend too much on the initiative of the disciple. A group-based approach overcomes this drawback and is a vital part of a church's discipling. There is, however, a recognition that many people require a type of discipling which deals with them as individuals, and which is a personal and private response to their needs, based on trust and relationship.

This has become a common form of one-to-one discipling. In this approach the disciple is assisted by a trusted adviser, such as a counsellor, a spiritual director, a pastoral supervisor, a senior friend or a soul mate. This more formal side of the discipling process needs to be backed up by a whole range of helpers and befrienders, organized and informal, long-term and short-term, specialist and general. A church needs to offer a full range of discipling which can meet the needs of all its members throughout their Christian lives.

Christian service

Discipling for Christian service, whether in Christian organizations or in secular employment, is an area which particularly requires the one-to-one approach. The disciple will need to be given an assessment of his or her personality and abilities, information about the different possible avenues of service, help in making decisions and applying for posts, and support when he or she finally begins the work in question. This is a personal and many-sided process, and it needs a secure and stable environment in which the issues can be discovered and developed.

In the area of Christian service it is far too easy to make crisis responses which lead to ill-considered and unhelpful decisions, based only on immediate needs or pressure from other people. A church needs to be discipling its members into their right places of work, rather than forcing or cajoling them into whatever vacancies arise in a crisis, only to be faced with similar crises a little later on because the people were not cut out to do those particular jobs. Often the investment of a little time and effort at this stage can prevent a lot of problems for the individual and the church at a later time.

Crisis discipling

Discipling or counselling in crisis situations will usually start on a one-to-one basis; only later will it take place within a help group or support group. Emergency response at the time of a disaster and in its immediate aftermath is generally best handled by one person or, at most, a few people and on a personal basis. Even the use of groups often needs an individual response alongside it. It is usually best for just one person to take a disciple through the short-term and long-term discipling they need. Continuity and co-ordination are of prime importance, and placing the overall responsibility for this in the hands of just one person generally works best. Care must be taken to define the boundaries between counselling and discipling, between social work and pastoral care. If crisis discipling does not eventually lead to discipling in the Christian life, the crisis will tend to recur in an ever more frequent and severe cycle.

Growing churches

Discipling has been recognized as one of the major factors in growing churches. Where there is good one-to-one discipling people become strong Christians, committed to the local church, and fully involved in Christian service. People are attracted to a church where they feel that any needs that they have or that might arise will be met in a compassionate and competent way. They are also attracted to a church in which they think they will be able to exercise the gifts and abilities which God has given them. So both potential disciples and potential disciplers need to see the church as a fellowship which emphasizes discipling.

Good discipling, however, is not only important in attracting new people and so helping the church to grow; it is also important in helping existing members to grow. It is sometimes thought that to emphasize the importance of discipling is to be too inward-looking or self-centred, but a right kind of discipling is exactly the opposite, for it produces mature Christians who can selflessly move out in service both inside and outside the church. There often needs to be an investment in discipling so that a return of healthy and functioning people can result. Churches which are willing to make such an investment will find that growth in numbers and character will follow.

Dying churches

Conversely, where such discipling is lacking or non-existent there is a slow death of the church, as its members become disillusioned and backslide or move elsewhere. They become disillusioned because they do not see the church doing what it should, valuing them as individuals; they backslide because they are neither receiving nor giving as they should; and they move elsewhere because they see the 'greener grass' of other churches which *are* doing what they should. The attitude which bypasses discipling, believing that other functions such as evangelism or social action are more important, results in a decline in which discipling is absent and so too are the other functions.

The vital work of the church in witness and service can only effectively be carried out from a base of strong and growing Christians, who are equipped and supported for this work. This does not mean that a church must wait until all its members are fully mature before it attempts any other activities. It does mean that discipling and these other activities must go hand in hand, so that first there is one step of discipling, then one step of outreach, and so on as the church moves forward. The 'foot' of discipling must be put forward first so that the other 'foot' of outreach can follow in step with it. Where discipling is omitted or neglected, the whole life of the church is affected adversely, so that it functions incorrectly and begins to die, its inner life waning and its growth outside wilting.

A specific example

Discipling at Stopsley Baptist Church includes all the aspects which we have already thought about in this chapter. We run one-to-one courses both for people who are interested in the Christian faith but have not yet made a commitment and for those who have recently become Christians and need some basic discipling. Our elders, deacons, housegroup leaders, youth leaders and children's workers are involved in one-to-one discipling, both for Christian living and service and for crisis situations. Individual church members help one another, both through friendships and in care groups. Sometimes people with particular needs are referred by the church to professional counsellors who can offer services such as marriage guidance, debt advice and career direction. The church provides training in a range of skills for leaders, befrienders, specialist helpers and disciplers. We try to encourage people to seek or offer discipling in any area of the Christian life and to support those who are involved in discipling others.

This emphasis on discipling at Stopsley Baptist Church was the result of both recognizing the needs of the congregation and the local community and discovering the gifts and abilities within the church. While the church provides a generalized, 'first-call' discipling service, it also specializes in parental discipling. The church has deliberately targeted this sphere of activity. We are able to run such a project because the local area (and hence the church) contains many families, and because we possess the necessary practical resources (such as a suitable building in which to hold meetings).

The planned future expansion of the church centres around new and redeveloped buildings and the opportunity which this will give us to offer regular one-to-one discipling to people, both within and outside the church. Facilities must be matched by a workforce to run them; training must be followed by real action; expansion must be backed up by resources; and our human ideas must be in line with God's will.

Part one in a nutshell

Disciples are followers, learners and imitators of Christ. We are all on a new journey. We need to be looked after, restored (like an old picture) and guided. The Bible contains many examples of people being helped in this way, 'discipled', with an emphasis on one-to-one, a discipler and a disciple. Some of these examples are wonderful, some are examples of how not to do it. In our contemporary situation we all need one-to-one help, not only at conversion, but throughout our Christian lives and especially in times of crisis. This kind of discipling can be decisive in the growth of a church and in the prevention of a church's death.

In the light of what has been said so far it would be well to pause and ask ourselves whether we need to take steps in our own fellowship or church to get something moving. Since one-to-one discipling is recommended in the Bible and is so obviously beneficial perhaps we should discuss the idea with the vicar, minister, elders, deacons, ministry team, readers, council members or whoever takes the lead in your church. If the idea is not turned down flat, go to the next section and begin to build up your case for the adoption of some kind of one-to-one scheme that would suit your particular church.

2

The 'Why?' of discipling

chapter four

The planting process

Jesus' parable of the sower (Matthew 13:1–23; Mark 4:1–20; Luke 8:1–15) shows us very clearly the need for discipling. If there is to be a harvest, then seed must be sown on soil that will yield crops. The fact that this is one of the few parables for which Jesus gives the twelve disciples an explanation tells us that it is of crucial importance for them. In explaining it Jesus reveals that he uses parables because the secrets of the Kingdom are meant only for those who are disciples; for others they are a mystery which they will not perceive or understand until they turn to God and are healed and forgiven (see Isaiah 6:9–10).

In the parable of the sower we can see several stages in the spiritual process of planting and growing.

Preparation

The sower is not defined in Jesus' explanation of the parable, but as the one who sows the Word of God he must be God himself, or his servants or both. It seems that the sower is God working through and with his people. Hence all disciplers are sowers. As God is the Chief Sower, so we are fellow-sowers with him, appointed by him and under his direction. Our task is to sow the seed of his Word, which he provides, in the field to which he sends us.

Like Isaiah, all disciplers are asked by God, 'Whom shall I send? And who will go for us?' And like him, they must answer, 'Here am I. Send me!' Then God can give them the instruction, 'Go and tell this people . . .' (Isaiah 6:8–9). They must dutifully sow the Word of God, whatever the response (or lack of response) to it may be. When Isaiah asks, 'For how long, O Lord?' God's answer is, in effect, 'Until it has achieved its result' (Isaiah 6:11–13).

Jesus, in his use of the harvest illustration, quotes the true saying, 'One sows and another reaps', and speaks of the sower and reaper being 'glad together' (John 4:36–37), reminding us that as sowers we are part of God's great work of producing a harvest crop for eternal life.

Sowing the seed of the Word of God is the responsibility of all Christians, as this quotation illustrates:

This is a story about four people named Everybody, Somebody, Anybody, and Nobody. There was an important job to be done and Everybody was sure that Somebody would do it. Anybody could have done it, but Nobody did it. Somebody got angry about that because it was Everybody's job. Everybody thought Anybody could do it but Nobody realized that Everybody wouldn't do it. It ended up that Everybody blamed Somebody when Nobody did what Anybody could have done!

The seed in the parable is the Word of God, and it is only when this is sown that a harvest can be produced. The Word of God is the truth of God spoken by the Father, the Son and the Holy Spirit. It is the Word which comes from the mouth of God: when God speaks, the thing that he has spoken happens (see Genesis 1). The Word of God is God the Son (see John 1:1–18). The Word of God is 'the sword of the Spirit' (Ephesians 6:17). It must not be limited to the Bible. The written Word is only part of the Word of God. God speaks in various ways – through the Scriptures, through the prophets, through his Spirit, and supremely through his Son (see Hebrews 1:1–2).

The discipler must use a variety of seed – that is, many different forms of the Word of God. Discipling must be the planting of God's Word into disciples' lives. This involves both directly quoting and reading Scripture and indirectly using biblical themes and truths. It is particularly helpful to point the disciple to the passages in the Bible which are the basis of the teaching which he or she is receiving from the discipler, and sometimes it is a good idea to get the disciple to read the passages aloud. This reassures them that you are really using Scripture and not just your own ideas. What the discipler believes to be the word of God for the disciple must always be tested against Scripture and by the Spirit.

The soils in Jesus' parable of the sower are people who are exposed to God's Word. Discipleship is the business of making disciples 'from every tribe and language and people and nation' (see Revelation 5:9; 7:9; 14:6). This is why one-to-one or person-to-person discipleship is so important, because it places the emphasis not on systems or groups but on individual people. Just as each soil is different and needs a different approach, so each person is different and needs a different method of discipling tailored to their particular needs.

The discipler is not to make superficial or selfish decisions about which soil is to be sown with the seed. The church has a duty to give all people an opportunity to hear; the gospel of the Kingdom must be 'preached in the whole world as a testimony to all nations, and then the end will come' (Matthew 24:14).

Just as the ultimate test of the soil is what it does to the seed, so people's lives are judged by how they respond to the Word of God. Just as digging and application of fertilizer can change useless soil into fruit-bearing soil (see Luke 13:6–9), so the discipler should be always trying carefully to cultivate the potential in the disciple so that he or she can become productive.

Sowing

Jesus told the disciples, 'The seed is the word of God' (Luke 8:11). This is a simple truth, and yet it is often forgotten. In the pressure to sow our denomination, our church, our self, our ideas, or a hundred and one other things, we can fail to sow the Word of God. Discipling can take on all the modern methods of education, interpersonal relationships and motivation, but if it lacks God's Word it is a fruitless exercise. We need to use a variety of appropriate ways of presenting the Word of God, but the message must never become subservient to the medium which is being used to communicate it. Too often it is the anecdote and not the point which is remembered. The disciple must not be left with just our

46

good presentation or clever illustration; through them he or she should have received God's Word. It is not the sack containing the seed but the seed itself which is important. Both Jesus and Paul point to the natural truth that the type of seed which is sown determines the type of plant which grows (see Matthew 7:16; Luke 6:44; 1 Corinthians 15:37–38). So in discipling, if the seed which we are sowing is just our own ideas, or other people's thoughts, then we will produce a crop of mere human ideas, but if we sow the Word of God we will produce a harvest of spiritual and eternal truth and life. We reap what we sow – either destruction through our sinful nature or eternal life from the Spirit (Galatians 6:7–8).

The sower in the parable was lavishly wasteful with the seed, literally broadcasting it all over the field. Discipling must be available with costly generosity to all people. We must be prepared for the seemingly wasteful sowing on three soils so that a crop can come from the fourth. Paul, in another context, reminds us that 'Whoever sows sparingly will also reap sparingly, and whoever sows generously will also reap generously' (2 Corinthians 9:6). We are not meant to sit counting each individual seed like misers; instead, we are meant to throw it on to the soil by the handful with abandon. The traditional emblem of the Bible Society was the Eastern farmer with an apron full of seed walking up and down a field, throwing the seed to the left and to the right. Similarly a radio or television signal is broadcast to every home in the reception area, even though only some of the radios and TVs will actually be tuned in to receive it. The discipler must take a similar attitude with the Word of God, taking a risk with it, trusting in the God who says, 'my word that goes out from my mouth . . . will not return to me empty, but will accomplish what I desire and achieve the purpose for which I sent it' (Isaiah 55:11). We must not limit our sowing to areas of guaranteed harvest results. Rather, with costly and sacrificial investment we must be prepared to sow without actually knowing what effect might be produced. And we have no guarantee that all our one-to-one discipling efforts will be rewarded with obvious success.

Germinating

In Jesus' parable we can see two main reasons for the lack of growth in the crop. First, the soil conditions were wrong – the seed fell on the path or on rocky ground. Secondly, the seed faced competition from the thorns.

Seed needs fertile soil combined with water and sunshine in order to grow and produce. Similarly, discipling must deal with the internal conditions of the disciple as well as the external conditions which they face – it must both renew the inner person and provide the right input. The disciple must be prepared in body, mind and spirit to receive God's Word. The God-given 'fertile soil' of the soul needs to be uncovered and exposed to the right amount of moisture and light: not so much that the soul is swamped or burned up, and not so little that the soul is parched or stunted. We must be careful not to attribute lack of germination to internal conditions when the cause is really external ones, or vice versa. Also, we must not blame the disciple or discipler when the problem is in fact caused by other factors.

Disciplers must be especially aware that because

48

British society has in recent generations become increasingly secular, much of the background Christian thinking which would have been present in a typical disciple's mind in previous generations is today absent. Many people today who are converted to faith in Christ are almost totally unfamiliar with the Bible – for example, they may not even know where Jesus was born. They may also lack an elementary knowledge of Christianity, such as understanding the meaning of Christmas or Easter. There may also be an absence of basic moral and ethical principles, such as believing that lying and stealing are wrong. Discipling will often need to start not just back at square one but many squares before that.

Seed must not only receive the right conditions but must also resist the wrong competition. Discipling must emphasize the positive but also address the negative. Plants die not only from lack of roots but also from the choking caused by weeds. Discipling must produce Christians who are strong in their own lives and able to withstand attacks from outside. Trouble and persecution, the worries of this life, the deceitfulness of wealth, and desires for other things are still the major reasons for lack of growth among Christians. Life's worries, riches and pleasures still cause Christians to fall away and to lack maturity. These issues must be addressed by the discipler with both negative warnings and positive alternatives. The disciple needs a list of 'You shall nots' and a list of 'You shalls'. And remember that the idea of 'shall' and 'shall not' may be offensive to the disciple as well as totally new. We can take nothing for granted.

Competition comes in many forms, not only in the obvious and blatant ones of secularism and satanism, but also in the disguised and subtle ones of religion and reason. The church itself can be a competitor against true discipling, and the culture of the society around us will certainly compete against a costly commitment to Christ. A radical following of Jesus will often be countered not by head-on opposition, but by an indirect questioning. It may be suggested to the zealous disciple that he or she is going to dangerous extremes and that Christianity is all right if it's done in moderation! The discipler must prepare the disciple to resist both the enemy from within and the enemy from without.

The discipler must also resist the temptation to mould the disciple into his or her own ways. Each of us has our own unique relationship with God and we cannot expect someone else to be a replica of ourselves, neither should we want it!

Gains and losses

Jesus said that the seed which fell on good soil 'came up and yielded a crop, a hundred times more than was sown' (Luke 8:8). Discipling brings gains for the two individuals involved, but also countless more gains to many others. The church is increased and strengthened, families and friends are influenced, the local community and the wider world are affected. Jesus speaks about a hundredfold return on the initial investment in discipleship. This may seem like an over-estimate, but if each one of us were to disciple one person per year, we could disciple say thirty people in a lifetime of ministry. And if each of them were also to disciple at the same rate, then the cumulative effect would be over thirty disciples in six years, over sixty in seven years, over a hundred in eight years, and so on!

The numerical return is only the tip of the iceberg, for God can accomplish an immeasurable amount of good through one person who is totally dedicated to him. Disciplers must remember that while church history concentrates on the famous, there is always behind them the unknown teacher, encourager, giver or pray-er without whom their ministry would not have been possible.

We should also remember that much that is now seen as gain will be shown in the light of eternity to be loss, and much that we feel to be loss will in fact be eternal gain. Our question, 'Lord, when did we see you . . .?' (Matthew 25:37, 44) can only be answered by his assessment that 'Whatever you did [or did not do] for one of the least of these brothers of mine, you did [or did not do] for me' (Matthew 25:40, 45).

Lack of belief, falling away and lack of maturity are unwelcome results. When they do come we must have the honesty to scrutinize our discipling for any failure. But we should also remember that even Jesus, the best discipler there ever was, saw some failures in his discipling. These were not his own fault, but the inevitable outcome of the decisions made by his disciples themselves. Even among the Twelve there was one who would be lost – Judas Iscariot (John 6:70–71). When many of his disciples turned back and no longer followed him, Jesus asked the Twelve whether they wanted to leave too, and Peter replied, 'Lord, to whom shall we go?' (John 6:66–69).

In our own discipling there may be many losses: many of the people whom we disciple may fail to come through to Christian maturity. But perhaps those losses count for less than the few disciples who remain.

Ezekiel, the 'watchman for the house of Israel', was accountable for losses when he did not speak out, but if he warned the people and they ignored him, then he was not accountable (Ezekiel 33:7–9). Paul, the apostle, was innocent of losses because he had 'not hesitated to proclaim. . . . the whole will of God' (Acts 20:26–27). We must wisely and faithfully carry out our God-given task of discipling others (see Matthew 24:45; 25:21, 23), for 'it is required that those who have been given a trust must prove faithful' (1 Corinthians 4:2).

chapter five

Guidelines for growth
Birth before growth

In order to grow, a Christian must first be born. We cannot disciple other people if we are not Christians ourselves. And if we are Christians, we cannot disciple those who are not Christians themselves. So one of the first tasks in any discipling is to make sure that both the discipler and the disciple really are Christians. This should never be assumed, even in the most obvious of situations. At some evangelistic events some of the clergy who had been counselling people became Christians there themselves! In discipling a person, we should be open to the possibility that the root cause of their needs could be a lack of Christian faith. Trying to produce spiritual growth in a non-Christian is as pointless as giving artificial resuscitation to a dummy!

When discipling people who say they have been a Christian for a while, a useful check is to ask them what they would say to another person who wanted to know what a Christian is and how to become one. It is important to distinguish between a real absence of spiritual birth in people and the mere *feeling* that they are not born again. They may indeed need to become a Christian, or they may already be converted but need the assurance that they really are a Christian. It is also helpful for the discipler to share his or her testimony, as this both assures the disciple of the discipler's Christian faith and makes clear to the disciple what a real Christian is.

The desire to grow

Growth only comes through a desire to grow. The child who has no desire to eat will not grow physically. The person who has no desire to learn will not grow mentally. The person who has no desire to love will not grow emotionally. The Christian who has no desire to be discipled will not grow spiritually. There needs to be a hungering and thirsting after righteousness. It is now recognized that the will to live is an important factor in achieving healing and recovery; the will to survive is essential in enduring imprisonment and solitude; and the will to succeed is necessary in overcoming opposition and handicap. Similarly, the disciple must have the will to live as a Christian, the will to survive against persecution, and the will to succeed against temptation.

So often in his healing miracles Jesus questioned people's desire to be healed, asking them what they wanted (Mark 10:51) or whether they wanted to get well (John 5:6). So in discipling the discipler must be asking the disciple what they want to achieve and if they really desire to grow. God promises to meet the desires of those who delight in him and fear him (Psalms 37:4; 145:19), yet so often we do not have things because we do not ask God for them (James 4:2). In discipling both disciple and discipler must have the desire, in the words of the missionary William Carey, 'to expect great things from God and attempt great things for God'.

The need for help

Growth only comes about with help. Children will grow only if others feed, educate and love them. Discipling rarely happens in solitude. The disciple can only grow with help, and the discipler can only give help when it is requested and accepted.

Jesus called his disciples so that they could be with him (Mark 3:14), not so that he could give them a training manual and tell them to get on with it, or so that he could enrol them on a correspondence course which they could do back home. So the discipling process is really a partnership, a task which is shared between the disciple and the discipler.

Discipling should always be seen as help which enables the disciple to *do*, rather than help which does it *for* him; help which breeds *interdependence* and not dependence or independence. In the words of the letter to the Hebrews, discipling is the 'work and the love' we have shown God as we 'have helped his people and continue to help them' (Hebrews 6:10).

Breathing

The Holy Spirit is the breath which gives us spiritual life. The risen Jesus breathed on his disciples and said, 'Receive the Holy Spirit' (John 20:22). The Holy Spirit is the breath of God who is breathed into us when we are born again and whenever we receive blessing from God. Part of the discipler's job is to teach the disciple how to inhale God's Spirit, and occasionally the discipler will need to do some emergency artificial respiration!

Anyone who has witnessed the birth of a baby knows how important that first breath is. But babies need to keep on breathing if they are to live, and when their babies are sleeping many parents worry about whether they are breathing properly or not. All Christians receive or inhale the Holy Spirit when they are converted (see John 3:5), but they need to keep on inhaling him if they are to live and grow spiritually (Ephesians 5:18). We must keep on breathing, for our previous breath has gone and is of no use for our present needs; similarly, the Spirit's filling must be continuous and ever new.

To breathe physically we need to expand our lungs, clear our windpipes and unblock our noses. Similarly, with spiritual breathing we need to deepen our devotion to Jesus and to remove any hindrances. Our intake of breath varies according to our circumstances: it is high when we are exercising and low when we are sleeping. Similarly, disciples must learn to alter their spiritual intake according to the amount they are expending.

Eating

The apostle Peter writes, 'Like newborn babies, crave pure spiritual milk, so that by it you may grow up in your salvation' (1 Peter 2:2). The 'milk' which Peter is referring to is the Bible. God's Word is also described as 'bread' (Matthew 4:4) and 'solid food' (1 Corinthians

3:2). Just as babies are taught to drink milk, so disciples must be taught to 'consume' the Bible – reading it, understanding it, learning it and obeying it. The child's progression from milk to solid food is an analogy for the disciple's progression from spiritual infancy to spiritual maturity.

Just as adults need a balanced and varied diet to be healthy, so the Christian needs input from both the Old Testament and the New; from the history books, the prophets, the wisdom literature, the gospels, the letters and Revelation; from both favourite passages and neglected ones; from both clear ones and obscure ones.

Our weekly food intake cannot be crammed into one massive Sunday lunch; neither can our Scripture input be packed into one solitary Sunday sermon. The discipler must show how vital daily Bible reading is and must give clear teaching on how to do it. The disciple needs to be given some practical help, such as guidance on when and where to read the Bible, what approach to adopt, which translation to read and, if applicable, which series of notes to use. Disciplers must lead by example, sharing with the disciple those things which they receive from their own daily reading of God's Word.

Exercising

Spiritual exercise or training, which 'has value for all things' (1 Timothy 4:8), is another vital ingredient for growth. The breath and food which the disciple takes in produce energy, and that energy must be used – otherwise the disciple will become feeble and flabby.

Football has been defined as 'thousands of people who

are desperately in need of exercise watching twenty-two men who are desperately in need of rest'. Sadly, a similar definition can be truthfully applied to the church. Too often all the work is done by a handful of committed people while the rest stand by and watch, either cheering or booing, as the case may be! Disciples must be encouraged to use their spiritual energy to train to do the work of God's Kingdom, and then to do it. Children are not told that they don't need to learn to walk simply because they cannot complete a marathon; similarly, we must not exclude disciples from God's work because they cannot run a large church! Jesus began by using his disciples to take messages, organize crowds, distribute food and provide pulpits; only later on did he tell them to preach the Kingdom of God, heal the sick and drive out demons.

The temptation with physical exercise is that we only do it out of a feeling of guilt or under duress from others. So with spiritual exercise, the disciple must be encouraged to adopt a regular pattern rather than to respond sporadically to calls to serve here or evangelize there. Like Timothy, we must not neglect our gift (1 Timothy 4:14) but must fan it into flame (2 Timothy 1:6).

Stunted growth

In a child lack of adequate nourishment can result in stunted growth, disease and death. Similarly, disciples who are malnourished can become stunted in their spiritual growth, lukewarm in their love for Jesus and even in danger of abandoning their faith altogether.

Many Christians seem to have gained the impression

that Christian growth is rather like human physical growth between the ages of eighteen and sixty, in which we develop all our adult faculties by the age of eighteen and only marginally refine them in the following years. But in fact Christian growth should be like physical growth between birth and the age of eighteen, with rapid progress and development throughout.

Discipling should always include an element of growth measurement and quality control, asking what progress there has been since last week, last month, or last year. The dramatic growth of the first few years of a child's life and the growth spurts of adolescence should find their parallels in spiritual growth. If the disciple seems not to have developed significantly in the space of a year, then there must be real concern about their Christian life. Progress should not be measured according to the standard of other Christians but according to the standard of God. That does not mean the discipler's vision of a perfect Christian, but God's plea for that particular person to be him or herself to the full.

It is all too easy for stunted growth to go unnoticed or to be accepted unthinkingly. It has its own alluring charm of ease and quiet. It is a downward spiral which starts with insufficient growth, then becomes an absence of growth, and finally, ends with negative growth or shrinkage.

Flabby growth

Some 'growth' gives the appearance of good development but is really only a mask. Discipling must look behind the mask and discover the real situation. Body builders who give up their training find that the muscle soon turns to flab. Discipling must be for all of one's life; giving up leads to decadent uselessness.

Jesus had his fair-weather disciples, and Paul mentions those who gave up when the going got tough. Flab may look like muscle, but effort and exertion soon show the difference. We should never desire persecution, but it is true that opposition rather than acceptance strengthens the church. Paul tells us that there are people who have 'a form of godliness' while 'denying its power', and we are to 'have nothing to do with them' (2 Timothy 3:5). Some people look like committed Christians, but when they face pressure their apparent commitment evaporates.

Perhaps both Judas and Demas gave the impression of good growth for quite a while before their treachery and desertion showed that it had been merely cosmetic (John 13:2; 2 Timothy 4:10). The process in which growth becomes flabby is a gradual one which often goes unrecognized for a long time, so the discipler must help the disciple to test their growth effectively to make sure that it is firm and real.

Growth or death

For the disciple there can be no standing still: either we grow or we die. The ultimate danger of both stunted growth and flabby growth is that they lead to death. Faith which is not growing eventually withers and perishes. Four of the churches in Asia in Revelation 2 and 3 were in danger of dying because they were not growing. The Ephesian church was dying because it had abandoned its first love and had fallen from a great height. The church at Pergamum was dying because it courted false teaching. The church at Sardis was dying because it had a reputation for being alive but was dead. The Laodicean church was dying because it was neither hot nor cold but lukewarm; it believed itself to be rich but was actually 'wretched, pitiful, poor, blind and naked'. To each of these churches Christ sent his angel with this simple message: Repent, or else the lampstand of the church will be taken away. Jesus was telling them to remain true to him, to strengthen what was left of their faith, which was in danger of dying, and to open the door to let him come in.

chapter s i x

Multiplying disciples

Then Jesus came to them and said, 'All authority in heaven and on earth has been given to me. Therefore go and make disciples of all nations, baptising them in the name of the Father and of the Son and of the Holy Spirit, and teaching them to obey everything I have commanded you. And surely I will be with you always, to the very end of the age.'

(Matthew 28:18–20)

'Go and make disciples . . .'

Jesus' command to go and make, baptize and teach disciples is sandwiched between his declarations that all authority is given to him and that he is with us always. The commission to make disciples must therefore be fulfilled with the presence and in the power of the risen Christ. Jesus' disciples were to wait in the city after his ascension until the Holy Spirit, the Spirit of divine power (Luke 24:49), was given to them. Only when the Spirit came did they begin the task of making disciples – 'three thousand' on the first day and then daily 'those who were being saved' (Acts 2:41, 47).

When the number of disciples became too great for the apostles to cope with, they appointed deacons to help in the task. As the number of disciples continued to increase rapidly (Acts 6:1–7), others who were neither apostles nor deacons became involved (such as Ananias, Priscilla, Aquila and Apollos).

The book of Acts is the record of the early Christians' response to Jesus' Great Commission. Filled with the power of the Holy Spirit they went out as Jesus' witnesses, beginning in Jerusalem, then reaching 'all Judea and Samaria' and, finally, going 'to the ends of the earth' (Acts 1:8). Sometimes the going was voluntary, at other times it was forced upon them by persecution (Acts 8:1, 4). But wherever they went, they preached the gospel and made disciples. As already mentioned the early believers were called 'disciples' before they were called 'Christians' (Acts 11:26). Perhaps this is an indication that their number one priority was to fulfil Christ's commission to go and make disciples.

Paul's great missionary journeys were really discipling campaigns; he spent his time making disciples and then strengthening and encouraging them (Acts 14:21–22). The Great Commission has never been rescinded because it will be in force until 'the very end of the age' (Matthew 28:20). So present-day Christians are meant to work under exactly the same mandate as the one which Jesus gave to the apostles.

Church growth

Church growth has been categorized under three headings: biological growth (members of Christian families becoming Christians); conversion growth (people outside the church becoming new Christians); and transfer growth (existing Christians from other churches joining, either because they are moving into the area or because they want a different kind of church). But ultimately there can be no church growth of any kind without *Christian growth*. Churches only grow when existing Christians develop and mature in their faith and as people are born again and become new Christians. Discipling is therefore at the heart of church growth and, indeed, at the very core of the church's existence.

In his ministry Paul recognized this link between discipling and evangelism. He told the Christians in the Corinthian church that as their faith continued to grow, his area of activity among them would expand and the gospel would be preached in the regions beyond their city (2 Corinthians 10:15–16). Their personal spiritual growth would have an impact firstly on the city of Corinth, as more and more people became Christians, and then would touch the surrounding province, as even more people were converted and new churches were formed.

Personal Christian growth leads to growth *in* the church, which in turn leads to growth *of* the church. A church may have a big membership, it may run exciting programmes, it may have large and well-equipped premises, but if the desire to see personal Christian growth leading to corporate church growth in new converts is not at the heart of everything it does, then the people will gradually leave, the programmes will eventually cease, and the premises will finally become obsolete. The twin commands of Jesus to make and teach disciples must be held together. A church which only makes disciples will die from infant mortality; a church which only teaches disciples will die due to a declining birth rate.

A chain reaction

> You then, my son, be strong in the grace that is in Christ Jesus. And the things you have heard me say in the presence of many witnesses entrust to reliable men who will also be qualified to teach others.
>
> (2 Timothy 2:1–2)

Paul's blueprint for discipling was a chain reaction in which he discipled Timothy (and others), Timothy (and others) discipled reliable people, they discipled others, and so on and so on. Even within the relatively short span of the history of the early church which is recorded in the New Testament (perhaps some seventy years), we see this process developing, so that by the end of the apostolic age (say the end of the first century) there were people in the church who could continue the discipling process, because they themselves had been discipled. The final picture we have of Paul at the end of Acts is of a man boldly preaching the Kingdom of God and teaching about the Lord Jesus Christ, a discipler to the very end, a man who would not be put off by those who would not believe (Acts 28:30–31).

As we have received teaching in the faith from a

'Paul', so we are to be 'Timothys' and teach others in our turn. We must ensure that the chain of discipling is not broken. Once a church ceases to continue this process, its days are numbered, for it becomes an ever-shrinking group whose whole effort is taken up with self-preservation and self-survival. On a personal level, if we fail to pass on what we have received we do not become richer, but poorer. In the parable of the talents 'everyone who has will be given more, and he will have an abundance. Whoever does not have, even what he has will be taken from him' (Matthew 25:29). The discipler's aim to make disciples must be instilled in the disciples as soon as possible, so that they will quickly be looking for others whom they can begin to disciple. Really the role of disciplers is to do themselves out of a job!

A graphic example of this is the chain of discipling which led to the conversion of Billy Graham. In 1858 a Sunday school teacher named Mr Kimball led a Boston shoe clerk called Dwight L. Moody to give his life to Christ. Moody became an evangelist, and in England in 1879 he awakened evangelistic zeal in the heart of one Frederick B. Meyer, the pastor of a small church. Meyer, preaching on an American college campus, brought to Christ a student named J. Wilbur Chapman. Chapman became involved in the YMCA and employed a former baseball player named Billy Sunday to do evangelistic work. Sunday held a revival campaign in Charlotte, North Carolina. A group of local men were so enthusiastic afterwards that they planned another campaign, bringing Mordecai Hamm to the town to preach. In this second campaign a young man named Billy Graham heard the gospel and yielded his life to Christ. One of the authors of this book heard and responded to the call to Christian ministry through Graham's preaching at the SPREE 1973 meetings in London.

At Spurgeon's Bible College he had the strange experience of being taught by one of his contemporaries at school! It must be an even stranger thing to be taught by one of your own students. Sometimes this will be the experience of the discipler, as the disciple matures in the faith and grows into his or her own teaching ministry. We need grace from God to let others move ahead of us or take over from us. Andrew needed it when Peter, the brother whom he brought to Jesus, became the leading disciple and apostle. Ananias needed it when Paul, the young convert whom he had taught and baptized, became the leading missionary. Disciplers should not expect their disciples to be their permanent students who will never progress to being teachers.

Equally, disciples must avoid allowing themselves to be for ever taught and never teaching. There is always the danger that those who by this time ought to be teachers in fact need someone to teach them 'the elementary truths of God's Word all over again' (Hebrews 5:12). One sign of Christian immaturity is the inability to become a teacher – always remaining a pupil, constantly soaking up but never giving out. At some level, we are all meant to move on from the classroom to the workroom, from being the receiver to becoming the giver. This is not meant to be a sudden or total process. The balance should gradually change so that we are always learning but increasingly sharing with others. Disciplers particularly face the temptation of finding their security in their discipling, wanting to keep their disciples dependent on themselves in order to meet their own needs. We need to heed the words of Paul that we should look not only to our own interests but also to the interests of others (Philippians 2:4).

Quantity and quality

Some Christians think that quantity is what matters in discipling, while others think that quality is more important. Should we be trying to get large numbers of people converted, or should we instead concentrate on a few and make sure that they grow up to be strong, mature Christians? But we should not try to choose between these two things, because they are both important. Jesus wants everyone to be saved and to have life to the full – he wants large numbers of converts who will all become mature Christians; he wants both quantity *and* quality. Mass evangelism has been defined as large numbers of people becoming Christians one by one, so 'mass discipling' is the one-to-one discipling of as many people as possible.

The large quantity of people (three thousand) who were saved on the day of Pentecost developed in quality as they devoted themselves to discipling (Acts 2:42–47). Due to that quality the Lord was able to increase the quantity of converts still further, as he added daily to their number. Acts records the growth of the church from 'three thousand' (Acts 2:41) to 'five thousand' (Acts 4:4) to 'many thousands' (Acts 21:20), with frequent other references to large numbers. Paul's aim was to 'present everyone perfect in Christ' (Colossians 1:28) – a goal of total numbers and complete excellence.

Discipling should not dodge the issue of measurement, either of quantity or quality, but should be prepared to make a realistic assessment which can show the reasons for failure and the causes of success. God is not against counting as such, as the inclusion of the book of Numbers in the Old Testament shows (Numbers 1:1–3), but is against counting when it is done with wrong motives and for manipulative purposes, which was David's sin in counting his fighting men (2 Samuel 24).

We should neither ignore numbers nor become obsessed by them. Measurement is a good servant but a bad master. Statistics can sometimes be misleading (indeed, they are often used dishonestly), so we must do our counting very carefully and assess its results 'with sober judgment' (Romans 12:3). We must avoid the sin of Ananias and Sapphira, who lied not only to people but also to God's Holy Spirit (Acts 5:1–11).

Quantity can be the enemy of quality. Discipling is not meant to be a mere production line, in which meeting quantity targets is the number one priority and quality control is neglected. We need to attempt the most *and* the best that we can achieve, with God's wisdom and help. Where should we invest our often limited resources? Should we spread them as thinly and widely as possible, or should we concentrate them in key areas? Jesus recognized the value of both quantity and quality, so he gave time to the crowds who wanted to hear his teaching as well as to the Twelve and to individuals. We need that sense of divine compulsion which drives us to do only what God wants us to do, without feeling guilt or superiority. If we are listening to God's voice, we can have the freedom to say 'yes' to some tasks and 'no' to others, to help one person even to the exclusion of some others.

Even quality needs measurement, because we can fool

ourselves and even others that what we are producing is top quality, when in fact it is second rate. Jesus severely judged the religious leaders of his day, particularly the Pharisees, who enjoyed position and influence but failed to fulfil their task. They did not practise what they preached; they did not carry the loads which they expected others to carry; they did not allow others to enter the kingdom of heaven, and when they won a convert they made him 'twice as much a son of hell' as they themselves were (Matthew 23:3–4, 13, 15): a sober judgment indeed.

The testing of quality must not be according to our own human standards but according to the standard of Jesus Christ, who will test the quality of each person's work (1 Corinthians 3:13). We are to 'aim for perfection' (2 Corinthians 13:11), both in our own lives as disciplers and in the lives of each person who is our disciple.

Part two in a nutshell

Jesus' parable of the sower, the seed and the soils gives us a fascinating parallel between husbandry and growing people and churches. People-growth needs preparation; sowing, germination, growth and harvest. At each stage we, as individuals, need a helper alongside us if as a fellowship we are to produce thirty, sixty or one hundredfold. Admittedly the majority of Christians have survived without one-to-one discipling, but how much better would we have been if we had had it? Spiritual growth can be compared to physical human growth too; breathing, eating, exercising, dying even, we all need each other. And thus the church will multiply by chain reaction, both in quality of life and in quantity of disciples.

So the reasons for one-to-one discipling become clear: because at every stage of our spiritual lives we need someone alongside us to help us through it and on to the next stage. Seen in this light it seems obvious, yet still the idea might be resisted because it is unfamiliar and we see problems. Do disciplers need training? Where will they find the time? What if disciples refuse to take part? These are genuine questions and need to be thought through before we embark on a programme of one-to-one discipling. But first let's consider the 'When?' question.

3

The 'When?' of discipling

chapter seven

Begin at the very beginning

The early days of a new Christian's spiritual life are of crucial importance, not only because he or she is most vulnerable then but also because the patterns laid down at the beginning have a profound influence on the rest of his or her Christian life.

The prime needs at this point are to establish, assure and protect: to establish the decision that has been made in the thoughts and actions of the new Christian; to assure them that the decision was real, even when there seems to be little to support that; and to protect them from Satan, from the church, and from themselves. Satan will try to undermine or destroy the new convert's faith; the church may overwhelm or disappoint them; and they themselves may be over-enthusiastic in some respects or may have deep doubts.

Discipling at this stage involves availability, support and understanding. The discipler needs to be an emergency service which is contactable and effective, a source of encouragement and practical advice, and a person who offers acceptance and discernment. Boundaries need to be drawn which define what 'availability' means, because people have differing ideas about what constitutes an emergency. Even at this early stage inter-dependence needs to be established rather than depen-dence or independence. New Christians have to learn to stand on their own feet, knowing that someone is there when they fall and is available to show them how to take more steps.

Real birth or still birth?

Two issues need to be addressed during this phase. First, was there a true spiritual birth or does there need to be further help to bring about conversion? Secondly, how can this new, vulnerable life be preserved and encouraged to grow? There is no point in trying to nurse what has not yet been born, nor in trying to bring to birth what has already been born. The Spirit's wisdom is needed to make the right assessments here. We should not question the reality of the new Christian's faith every time he or she voices a doubt or fails to grasp a truth; neither must we rush forward regardless, refusing to even consider the possibility that this disciple may not actually be a Christian yet. Preserving a new Christian life requires protection and encouragement combined with sensitiv-ity and firmness.

Television nature programmes often show how vulnerable young animals are to predators, and young Christians are similarly at risk. There will be decisions at this stage which we will need to take for new converts and actions which we will need to encourage them to do. This first phase will need a highly directive approach because of the great dependency and vulnerability of the new disciple. Just as some new-born babies progress well almost from the moment of birth while others may need to be nursed in intensive care, so we must discern the particular needs of each new Christian.

Personal or organizational?

For a new Christian, like a new baby, the most important thing is having his or her own needs met rather than being integrated into the family or community. Discipling at this stage must therefore centre on the person rather than on organizations. We tend to laugh at parents who discuss which schools and universities their new-born babies will eventually attend, what careers they will pursue, whom they will marry, and how many children they will have! However, there is a danger that we may rush our new Christians into similar discussions and considerations at far too early a stage. A new baby's basic needs are to be loved, fed, cleaned and allowed to sleep. So new Christians must know that they have loving care and concern, access to teaching, acceptance when they go wrong or do not understand, and (in the midst of all our eagerness and their enthusiasm) time to rest. Too many new Christians end up getting dizzy on the merry-go-round of meeting every church member and going to every church group. The discipler must be willing to suspend some of their hectic activity to give unhurried quality time to their new disciple. Like Jesus, the discipler needs to go up on a mountain with the disciple (Mark 3:13).

A Christian or a 'church-ian'?

The new convert must initially see himself or herself as
a Christian person rather than a church person. There is
a danger that this early discipling may concentrate too
much on church life and too little on the Christian
faith. Church information and integration can follow
later, once the new believer has sufficient inner
resources to face the outward responsibilities of church
membership. Explanations of the differences between
the denominations or a crash course in our church's
constitution are not what is required at this stage! Paul
said that what was 'of first importance' for the new
Christian was 'that Christ died for our sins . . . that he
was buried, that he was raised on the third day' and
that he appeared to hundreds of people (1 Corinthians
15:3–6).

The crucial first period

The vital first stage of discipling quickly leads into a
more extended opening phase. While the discipling may
become less intense, it is still just as important.
Commitment is required from both the discipler and
the disciple. While foundations may not have a very
high visible profile, they are crucial if a stable building
is to be erected. Disciplers must have a clear idea about
what ground they want to cover in this period, and they
need to keep asking themselves why they are covering
this or that particular subject. It is a good idea to use
prepared material, either from one's own church or from
a wider organization (see *Resources* p. 157 for examples),

as this gives disciples the confidence that they are being given the general teaching of the church rather than being indoctrinated into their disciplers' own personal views.

Constant reference should be made to the Bible, as this gives an objective standard for information and discussion. The disciple must have his or her own Bible in an appropriate translation and must be shown how to use it. Like Jesus on the Emmaus Road, we need to begin 'with Moses and all the Prophets' and explain 'to them what was said in all the Scriptures' about Jesus (Luke 24:27) and, like Philip on the desert road, we need to begin with a passage of Scripture and tell them 'the good news about Jesus' (Acts 8:35). What is done in this opening period sets the scene for much of what will follow in the discipling process.

A basic course in Christianity

The early phase of discipling needs to be like a basic course in Christianity. In a sense this is a 'crash-course' but we should take care not to overwhelm a person new to the faith with too much new material to learn all at once. Remember, it may all be quite unfamiliar. However, priorities in the disciple's life need to be identified; they must receive some foundational teaching; a pattern of personal devotions needs to be established; they must begin to live a Christian lifestyle. Space must be given for both the convert's questions and the discipler's answers. A balance needs to be achieved between what the new Christian asks to know and what he or she needs to know. Questions must not be ignored, but the discipling must not be limited to those questions. This phase of discipling must establish both a reserve of knowledge and a range of skills; it must introduce the disciple to Christian doctrine and Christian living. Decisions about what ground to cover at this stage must be shaped by both the immediate and future needs of the disciple. As in Paul's letters, there must be both theory and practice, what disciples need to know and what they need to do.

The teaching which the disciple receives during this period will form a basic reference library and instruction manual for his or her Christian life. As far as circumstances and intellectual ability allow, the disciple needs to personalize the teaching material by looking up and reading Bible passages, taking notes, and doing their own reading and study between sessions with the discipler. Bottle feeding must give way to the disciple feeding himself or herself with solid food. The frequency of the meetings and the length of the course depends upon the disciple's availability and needs, although they need to show some commitment and self-discipline. The discipler must be willing to share his or her beliefs and lifestyle, so that the disciple, like Paul's prótegé Timothy, will know all about the discipler's teaching and way of life (2 Timothy 3:10).

But again, it is most important not to rush this early stage of learning. Familiar truths (familiar to the mature Christian) may be quite new and difficult to grasp for the new disciple. A rapid survey of Christian doctrine is unlikely to be understood. A lot of patience, care and love are needed.

An ever-widening circle

While the discipler is pivotal in this process, there must be an increasing involvement and input from others in the church. The information and integration which were referred to earlier are now appropriate and essential. The new Christian must begin to understand that commitment to Christ involves commitment to his people, that a Christian person needs also to be a church person. The discipler needs to suggest which meetings the disciple might attend and should integrate them into such groups. The discipler also needs to be establishing relationships between the disciple and a variety of other people in the church, both those to whom the disciple would naturally gravitate and those to whom they would not.

The new Christian in the church needs also to be the new Christian in the community. Faith must be applied to family and friends, work and play, possessions and finance. The discipler should be aware of the disciple's contacts and should perhaps be involved in some of them. This is particularly important with regard to the disciple's family, especially if they are not Christians. There may be other Christians or even a Christian group at their place of work, and they need to be introduced. Other Christians may share their hobbies and interests, and this can form a natural link and support. Expertise and experience from other Christians can be made available to them. This process should not isolate the new disciple in a Christian ghetto but should help them in their non-Christian environment.

Baptism or confirmation

Whatever form of Christian initiation is followed in a church, this needs to be explained to the convert during the early discipling, and the importance of an outward expression of the inward reality of his or her new faith should be emphasized. The discipler may carry out the preparation for this, or it may be done by someone else who does it for all the church's candidates. Particularly if the latter is the case, the discipler must continue to be as fully involved as possible. The discipler is an obvious person to be part of the initiation ceremony through prayer and the laying on of hands or in some other appropriate way.

Where the form of the initiation is believer's baptism by immersion, the belief being expressed needs to be clear and the meaning of the baptism needs to be fully understood. The belief in question is the Christian gospel or good news. Put very succinctly, this is the gospel message: God's plan of abundant life (John 3:16; 10:10); our problem of separation through sin (Romans 3:23; 6:23); God's remedy, the cross of Christ (Romans 5:8; 1 Peter 3:18); and our response, which is to receive Christ (John 1:12–13). The basis of the rite of baptism is our belief in Christ (Matthew 28:19; Romans 6:4), our conversion to Christ (Colossians 2:12), our cleansing by Christ (1 Peter 3:21), our consecration to Christ (Galatians 3:27), and our commitment to the church of Christ (1 Corinthians 12:13; Ephesians 4:5). *Being Baptized* by Stephen Gaukroger (Marshall Pickering, 1993) is a helpful guide to believer's baptism.

Where the form of the initiation is confirmation, the belief and basis will be similar, with the element of confirming all that was promised and potential in the earlier baptism. *Your Confirmation* by John Stott (Hodder, 1991) is a helpful handbook about confirmation.

Only a starting-point

Initiation is not a destination but a starting-point; it is a beginning, not an end. The disciple must have enough understanding for the ceremony to be meaningful, but does not need a degree in theology!

The public witness should not be unduly delayed. It is a statement of a past event (that is, the person becoming a Christian), of a present reality (that is, the fact that they are a Christian now), and of a future desire to be a Christian. What lies beyond the initiation is of crucial importance; it is helped but not guaranteed by the ceremony. The initiation must be a prelude to leaving the elementary teachings about Christ and going on to maturity, which, God permitting, the disciple will do (Hebrews 6:1–3). The outward disciplines of Bible study, prayer, fellowship and worship, and the inward disciplines of faith, consecration, obedience, surrender and dependence are the means of keeping one's relationship with Christ right.

We must respect the integrity of new disciples so that they can take part in the ceremony with meaning, but we must not overload them with a set of exacting requirements which prevent them from ever reaching it. What this specifically means for each new Christian will need to be agreed between them and their discipler, with the church leadership. We must not spoil the event either by rushing into it or by delaying it needlessly.

A birth announcement

If the new Christian waits until he or she feels ready for the initiation rite, they will probably wait for ever. It is a birth announcement and should come as close to the event of birth itself as possible. There may be issues to do with relationships and lifestyle which need to be resolved beforehand, and this can take time to achieve. There will be the organizational restraints of the particular church in arranging the occasion. All these things, however, should not be allowed to prevent the ceremony from being a wonderful expression and glorious celebration of new life. Some of the implications of the initiation will have to be left in abeyance, with the ceremony being a pledge to work at them.

Sometimes Christians in the early church would come to baptism wearing an outer garment which spoke of their past life. Perhaps it was a uniform or an outfit that was part of a now inappropriate lifestyle, or simply dirty and torn clothes which signified the wrong and failings of the past. These outer clothes were taken off as they went into the water, and new, clean white garments were put around them as they came up out of it. They knew that the implications of that statement had to be worked out the next day at home, at work and in their community. It was a statement of intent that being born again would result in a different life. Initiation needs to be that kind of declaration, announcing that from now on business will not be as usual, because the person is now under new management.

Baptism or confirmation thus marks the beginning of the committed Christian life. Discipling does not end at this point. All too often a young believer makes the public statement and with a sigh of relief at having 'arrived' sinks gently back into the old life in the illusory assumption that there is no further progress needed. But baptism and confirmation are initiations, not passing out parades. We turn now to the need for ongoing discipling. It is good, and often exciting, to take the plunge but then comes the hard slog of the swim!

chapter eight

Every part of life

The discipling process begins with conversion but is not limited to it. It is a process for every part of the Christian life. In this chapter we will look at discipling in three vital aspects of life: work, relationships and pressure.

The world of work

The disciple's work is a crucial area of his or her life which fundamentally affects time and money, family and friends, church and faith. Part of the discipler's role is to help the disciple to make the right choices and decisions in this area.

Most churches will possess a wealth of career expertise and experience, since their members will have done a wide variety of jobs. This needs to be shared on a one-to-one basis so that the disciple's crucial decisions about his or her education and career can have a Christian perspective.

With respect to education, special care should be taken to avoid the 'perpetual student syndrome', that is, education for education's sake. Advice should be given about the different values of general education (e.g., a university degree) and specific education (e.g., an apprenticeship); and also about the short-term and long-term worth of particular courses which are related to the present and expected labour market. Discipling in this area will need to vary greatly, depending on whether the disciple is a young person just starting working life or an older person looking for a complete change of career.

Discipling needs to balance the preferences and potential of the disciple with the possibilities of the job market. It will sometimes be the role of the discipler to suggest totally new areas, perhaps especially those which Christians do not usually enter or which have very few Christians in them. The disciple must be challenged to think through his or her expectations of work. What level of income do they want? How much job satisfaction and job security are they looking for? What kind of promotion potential, pension entitlement and fringe benefits do they expect? Do they want to serve others? What limitations would they put on their work, such as the hours involved, the distance they would have to travel, and the periods they would have to spend away from home? Are there moral question marks attached to some of the jobs they are considering, such as Sunday trading or exploitative working conditions?

Full-time Christian work is a more obvious area for discussion in discipling, but for that very reason it needs careful handling. In many churches there is an inbuilt bias towards this sector of work and away from industry, commerce and business. We need to be alert to the lure of the high status given to full-time Christian work within the church culture. Discipling in this area must address the realities of the situation and offer impartial advice.

While it may be appropriate for one person to handle this aspect of discipling for a particular disciple, they must call upon all the resources available to them. This will include individuals with special skills and background, as well as the back-up of Christian and secular organizations. Thought should be given to personality and aptitude tests as well as the possibility of work experience.

It is particularly important in this area to suggest trying out specific jobs, perhaps through voluntary work or short-term appointments in the field involved. In a difficult employment market there is a temptation to see full-time Christian work as an easy solution, but this temptation must be avoided for the sake of the individual concerned, for the sake of the work being contemplated and the people who might be harmed by a wrong decision taken at this level.

A further aspect of discipling in this area is guidance for those who are moving out of full-time Christian work into other types of employment. The factors here are often complicated by major changes such as moving to a different country.

Unemployment and retraining may also need to be dealt with in the discipleship process. Discipling must address the negative experiences of life as well as the positive ones. There must not be such an emphasis on work and vocation that the needs of the unemployed are neglected. While the whole Christian fellowship should seek to offer practical help to people who are experiencing unemployment, such times can also be a valuable opportunity for the individual to reassess their direction and find new avenues of activity and service. Retraining involves not only advice and support in gaining new skills for a new job, but also the retraining of attitudes and motives. A particularly hard decision is when to jettison a past type of work and to accept retraining for a new type.

It is important for the discipler to deal with the feelings of worthlessness and rejection by God and others which so often accompany unemployment. In such times the person needs to find self-worth and self-value in a source other than the work which they have done in the past. The discipler needs to show real interest, care and concern, but without seeming to be intrusive or burdensome.

Discipling in this area becomes more difficult as the length of the period of unemployment increases. Eventually most of what needs to be said will have been said, and then the discipler simply needs to sit and wait with the disciple. Abandonment at this stage might well be interpreted as betrayal. The discipler will need more than human patience.

The realm of relationships

With respect to personal friendships, the discipler's role is not to tell the disciple who his or her friends should be, but rather to give the disciple help to make wise choices. Some disciples will need to improve their interpersonal skills, that is, how to relate to others and communicate with them. The discipler will need to teach the disciple the biblical standards for friendships. Friendship is one of the areas that has the greatest potential for either fulfilment or disappointment. The old saying that it is better to have loved and lost than not to have loved at all highlights the dilemma. Sometimes, while those who are without a friendship are madly trying to find one, those who are in a friendship are just as madly trying to get out of it!

Discipling here should primarily seek to address the principles involved and to give the disciple the ability to face issues and make decisions. Only very rarely should the disciple get drawn into assessing the suitability of potential friends. Otherwise he or she too easily becomes the matchmaker to ensure that things go right or the scapegoat when things go wrong. This is particularly a sphere where the discipler needs to 'rejoice with those who rejoice' and 'mourn with those who mourn' (Romans 12:15). As well as dealing with aspects of friendship in which a disciple may ask for discipling, the discipler should perhaps also address the disciple's need to broaden their ideas and experience of friendship or their need to deepen their view and expression of friendship. In other words, the discipler may need to raise the issue as well as respond to the disciple's questions.

Family life is another sphere in which discipling is important, dealing with such issues as marriage and parenting, separation and bereavement. While discipling will inevitably tend to concentrate on problems, it must not be seen as exclusively problem-oriented. Marriage discipling, for example, needs to be making good marriages better as well as mending broken marriages.

The most common causes of tension in the home are related to communication, finance, emotions and relationships. Communication problems include literally not finding time to talk to one another, preaching or pontificating instead of communicating; trying to communicate with crossed wires and mixed messages; and hypocrisy – 'What you *are* or *do* speaks so loudly that I cannot hear what you *say*.' Finance problems will include having either too little or too much money. Emotional problems will include feelings of guilt, anger, hate or apathy which are either not expressed or not resolved. And relationship problems will have arisen because the relationship in question is either morally wrong in some way or is under stress for some reason.

All these causes are compounded by the twentieth-century backcloth of acceptable and easy divorce, widespread illegitimacy, the increasing absence of one parent and the inaccessibility of grandparents. The discipler must be always trying to get below the surface issues to the real ones, from the individual-centred ones to the family-centred ones. They must also try to administer preventive medicine rather than emergency first aid. Many of these situations will require specialist counselling and technical advice, but this still leaves a role for the discipler who can supplement this help with support and availability. In addition, the discipler can deal with matters when they are still at the irritation stage, long before they become a crisis.

Another important area of discipling is helping the disciple to cope with conflict and hostility in relationships. Key questions here will be, when should the disciple avoid conflict and when should they confront it? Who is causing the problem – the disciple or the other person? Why does the conflict arise? What should the disciple do to resolve it? Often it simply needs someone from outside to bring an independent perspective into a situation to which the disciple is too close to be able to see it clearly. Sometimes the most obvious question or statement suddenly brings the whole conflict into focus and provides a way to resolve it. The discipler will seek both to bring reconciliation where that is possible and to offer support where reconciliation is not possible. Through discipling some foes will become friends, others will not, and the disciple will require help in handling both.

As in so many other areas, the discipler will hope to anticipate difficulties rather than merely react to them when they arise. The discipler should help the disciple to adopt new attitudes and acquire new abilities which will enable him or her to avoid potential conflict. Jesus said we are to love our enemies (Matthew 5:44), but he also said we should leave those who will not welcome us or listen to us (Matthew 10:14), even when they are fellow Christians (Matthew 18:15–17).

Periods of pressure

Today stress is a significant factor in many people's lives. The discipler should understand that in any stressful situation in the disciple's life there will be a *source* of stress which causes a *reaction* of stress. The source must be identified – is it the disciple's work, church or home, or is it society in general? – and it must be graded as to its size and scale of impact. The nature of the reaction depends on the source of the stress and the disciple's perceptions of its impact – in other words, input plus interpretation. The effects of stress (called strain) can be mental, physical, psychosomatic (that is, both mental and physical), spiritual, or just vague.

Strategies for coping with stress include identifying

the source, the reaction and the effect; avoiding the avoidable and minimizing the unavoidable; managing the stress through purposeful planning; accepting the true support of groups and individuals and rejecting the false support of alcohol, nicotine, caffeine and other drugs; and changing one's personal lifestyle, self-image, attitudes and perceptions. Preventative strategies include ensuring physical fitness through exercise, weight-watching and eating healthily; maintaining one's physical and mental health through appropriate rest, relaxation and routine; developing a right self-image by rejecting 'poor me' (that is, self-pity, defeatism etc.), accepting the 'real me' (warts and all!), and cultivating 'God's me' (a new, forgiven, transformed person who increasingly resembles Jesus; see 2 Corinthians 5:17); and developing biblically-based attitudes towards our priorities in life, our perceptions of the world around us and our planning for the future.

There is a three-point process in coping with stress: first, I *can* cope with it; secondly, I *want* to cope with it; and thirdly, I *will* cope with it. The discipler will want to surround this strategy with biblical teaching about the redemption of one's whole person, the renewal of one's mind and the refinement of one's motives. The discipler should emphasize that Christian living is all about pleasing God by seeking to do his perfect will.

Change can be particularly stressful, and, therefore, there is a special need for discipling at times of transition. Changes involving people, places, plans, priorities and possessions create pressure and uncertainty. Changes in relationships with people can cause instability and can make disciples question their own role and value, especially if they have invested a lot in those relationships. Moving to a different place can create a sense of restlessness and not belonging, and can raise the awkward question, 'Where next?' Alterations to plans may produce disappointment or feelings of powerlessness in which the disciple seems like a very small pawn on a gigantic chessboard. Differences in priorities may cast doubt on previously held convictions and may cause fear about future ones, even to the point of wondering if anything can be trusted or relied upon. Changes in possessions can produce concerns about coping with either poverty or wealth.

The disciple's shifting world may be further complicated by changes in the discipler's own life, and hence in the relationship between the two of them. The disciple must learn to rely primarily on God and not on the discipler, or anyone else or anything else. Really there is change and decay in everyone and everything around us, and we can only have security when we depend upon the God who never changes.

The ultimate change is that of suffering loss, and this brings with it the greatest stress of all. The disciple who has suffered the loss of status or security needs all the support that a discipler can give. The response to loss depends on the personality of the one facing it, the nature of the loss, and the social environment. Each of these things needs to be addressed in discipling, and the process of coming to terms with the loss needs to be continued to its completion.

The disciplers need to know or get to know the disciple well enough to understand what it is in their character that makes them react to loss as they do. They need to understand the full extent of the loss, both factually and in the perception of the disciple. Then they need to become aware of the influences surrounding the disciple which either increase the intensity of the loss or help to lessen it. No two situations, however similar they may seem on the outside, are ever the same to the different people concerned, and the discipler should never seek to help by saying how someone else coped or by trying to equate this situation with another – even one they have experienced themselves.

chapter nine

Continue to the very end
Retirement and old age

As discipling continues throughout life, so it begins to
address the concerns which the concluding chapters of
life bring. Retirement marks a fundamental change in
lifestyle, and a discipler can encourage an honest look at
all that is involved. Preparation for retirement has
become a major concern of government and industry,
especially as more and more people take early retirement.
Christian discipling needs to address the practical
concerns, but also the emotional and spiritual ones. The
church fellowship can be a resource offering valuable
services to those in retirement and old age. The
traditional senior citizens' activities often cater only for
women, but they can be developed to cater for men also,
and to meet not only spiritual needs but also social and
physical ones.

One-to-one discipling will need to realistically face
the fears and apprehensions which this phase of life can
bring, to provide factual information or at least point to
where it can be obtained, and also to address the
emotional and spiritual needs that arise. In retirement

these are mainly needs related to self-worth and self-esteem. Those who have found significance and fulfilment in their job need to be shown other areas of living which can bring this sort of return. The feeling of having been left on the scrap-heap can only be overcome by finding acceptance and value from God through the attitude of others. Old age also brings feelings of helplessness and hopelessness. One emotive subject which may need to be dealt with in discipleship is that of euthanasia, which will require not just a biblical response but also emotional support and reassurance. Discipling at this phase must address the needs of the body, the mind and the spirit, and the need to continue growing in maturity in each of them.

Marriage discipling is not just for newly-weds, but can be helpful at every stage, including old age. As the ingredients and constituents of marriage change, so the partners may need help to adjust to these changes. The topics of communication, physical and sexual expression, and faithfulness all need to be dealt with in a way appropriate to the situation. Where the couple cannot meet each other's physical needs due to weakness or disability, understanding and support must be given, especially where they face loss of privacy. Marriage should be seen as a developing relationship in which some facets may become less important while others may take on a new priority.

Family relationships also need advice, especially as they are fundamentally changing during these closing chapters of life. The empty nest syndrome may have been first faced a number of years previously, but the implications of it become more acute in retirement and old age. It is hard no longer to be the dominant generation within the family, and especially to become more like the 'children' of your children in your dependence on them. Distance and personal differences make closeness difficult to maintain, but the effort needs to be encouraged, not only with children but also with grandchildren and great-grandchildren. Where contact with their own family is impossible for the disciple, the discipler may be able to arrange for them to adopt and be adopted by another family in the church.

Discipling also needs to address the area of friendships, and the discipler should offer the disciple practical help in forming them. This is often most difficult for the recently widowed, who have been used to relating to their friends as part of a couple. Questions may also be raised about the appropriate depth of friendships between elderly single people and members of the opposite sex. Sometimes the discipler can offer practical help by arranging social events for older people, or by suggesting or actually making contact between particular people. Difficulties in forming friendships in old age are often a combination of the legacy of the past, where this has been a problem, and the particular current situation, which creates obstacles. The discipler must tackle both of these with the disciple.

Illness and disability

To be a discipler who comes alongside someone in illness and disability is a demanding and yet rewarding role. It is just as important to be there with the person as it is to say or do anything. Hours spent at a home or a hospital bedside holding a person's hand are a costly yet vital expression of discipling. Care must be taken not to exploit the person's vulnerability, treating them as a captive audience, or outstaying one's welcome or violating their wishes. Particular thought should be given to spiritual ministries such as saying prayers, reading Scripture, hymns or songs, the laying on of hands, sharing in bread and wine, and anointing with oil, which should only be done with the person's agreement. Disciplers should never go beyond their competence or knowledge, especially in medical matters, and they should always respect the prior claims of the close family and professional carers.

Difficult questions concerning suffering and death should not be avoided, but the discipler should be ready to admit that he or she does not have all the answers. They should not be shocked by words or actions which are totally out of character; they should always be sensitive to the strain and stress the person is experiencing. Fears should be treated compassionately and realistically, neither playing them down nor blowing them up.

Alongside spiritual and emotional discipling there needs to be practical help, either performed or arranged by the discipler, which could include housework, gardening, maintenance, shopping, transport and entertainment. When offering help on behalf of others, the discipler should never make promises unless he or she is sure that these can be fulfilled. It is generally better to find out what is possible before suggesting it to the disciple.

Physical illness produces tremendous pressures, but generally this is even more the case with mental illness. This makes discipling even more demanding, because the usual means of rational communication may not be available and because the mental illness will often be accompanied by religious overtones of sin and failure. The discipler in this area will need a deep reservoir of personal resources and the special support of other Christians.

Financial problems

The reduction in income which later life often brings calls not only for financial advice but also for the sense that someone is willing to listen and understands the pressures. While we are not to serve money (Matthew 6:24), and to love it is a 'root of all kinds of evil' (1 Timothy 6:10), it is the key to so much of the material and physical world. Financial discipling in retirement and old age involves examining income, money management and expenditure control. Income can come from wages, pensions, state benefits, entitlements, investment interest, savings and gifts – all these sources need investigating. Money management involves investments, capital, property and insurance, each of which should be assessed where appropriate. Expenditure control involves budgeting, spending analysis, savings and economies. It is perhaps the most neglected area of financial management. In old age it may not be possible to change income or to capitalize investment, so the only area that can be varied is expenditure.

Disciplers may have some general financial knowledge, but should also be able to refer the disciple to other people with specialist knowledge. They have a responsibility both for the information they give personally and for that given by the specialists. A useful and illuminating question for disciplers to ask themselves is, 'Would I be happy to entrust my own financial affairs to the person whom I have recommended to my disciple?'

In addition to financial guidance, disciplers will need to advise the disciples about their views concerning money, their feelings about their financial situation, and any influences that affect their ability to correctly handle their financial affairs. These questions will not only be of a purely economic nature. For example, the disciple may apparently be angry about his or her financial situation, but the anger may, in fact, have a much deeper root and really be to do with the difficulty of coping with growing old. Symptoms, especially monetary ones, must not be confused with causes; otherwise the discipler will waste a lot of time trying to help to solve apparent problems which are really only expressions of the real, deeper problems.

Bereavement

Partners or close family members or friends may in one sense have been the nearest disciplers that a person had, so when they die another discipler needs to come alongside. Bereavement counselling is a specialist area which needs trained people, but there is a separate discipling function for a caring helper or befriender who clearly recognizes the differences between carer and counsellor and who acknowledge the limitations of the discipling process.

The stages of grief have been defined as denial and isolation (or despair and withdrawal), followed by anger, then bargaining, then depression, and finally acceptance. These are not neatly arranged chapters with a beginning and an end, but rather a series of images which fade from one to another. The discipler needs to be aware of this general pattern, but should not see discipling as a course which leads systematically through the five stages.

In bereavement discipling in old age there may be the added factor of the disciple's own acute fear of death, heightened by their contemporaries dying around them. So preparation for death may need to be part of this discipling. The way in which Jesus comforted Mary and Martha after the death of their brother Lazarus (John 11:17–37) provides a good pattern for bereavement discipling. Jesus allowed the sisters to express their questions, doubts, fears and anger, and he responded with his own appropriate statements, questions, clarifications and challenges – and all this within a framework in which emotions were admitted and openly shown by the sisters and by Jesus too. There needs to be a right balance between the emotional involvement of the discipler, which demonstrates their sympathy and empathy, and the emotional detachment which allows them to be a firm foundation and sure support.

Bereavement discipling is especially hard when there is uncertainty over the Christian standing of the person who has died. The discipler must avoid categorical statements about the person's eternal destiny, but must also be sensitive to the particular fears which the disciple may have. In all bereavement discipleship it is not the discipler's task to try and change what has happened but to help the disciple to cope with the reality of their situation.

103

Death

Preparing for dying and the sharing of the last moments of life are an awesome responsibility, but one that a discipler should not ignore. Having been helped at every other phase of life, the disciple should be helped now to conclude his or her earthly discipleship. The discipler can perform a very valuable role in the last moments of the disciple's life, supporting and encouraging them and finally dismissing them to God's presence in heaven. It is an amazing experience to be with a Christian when he or she dies.

In this discipling there should always be a clear and full recognition of the rights and wishes of the one who is dying. These must never be violated by the enthusiasm, ignorance or imposition of the discipler. Obviously, such a ministry to the dying disciple can only take place where the family understand it and fully welcome it.

The discipler should make sure that neither they themselves nor others try to decide what is best for the dying person without first seeking their opinion. Where this cannot be done, the discipler, based on what they know about the person, should try to imagine what they would be saying if they were able to. Spiritual ministry at this time should be in a form which is appropriate and acceptable for both the disciple and the discipler; it should not be imposed by others' traditions or expectations. Disciplers should remember that it is generally the sense of hearing which is the last faculty to go, and care should be taken about what is said in the presence of an unconscious person, because they may still be able to hear and understand. The final words which are said to the dying disciple need to be primarily words of assurance that the past is acceptably completed and the future is totally assured in Christ.

Both prior to the death and once it has taken place, the discipler has a responsibility to the other people who have been involved or have witnessed it. This obviously includes family and friends, but it may even involve other carers such as young nursing staff who may never have seen a death up to this time. After doing all that they can at the time of the death, the discipler should be aware of any help which people may then need to cope with the impact of what has happened, and should try to enable them to find that help.

Part three in a nutshell

Because discipling involves learning we easily fall into the trap of thinking that it is for young people or new Christians only. Certainly discipling at the beginning of the pilgrimage is vital. New Christians need help to be assured that they are truly born again; to understand the bases of the faith, but not to be overwhelmed by them; to join the church but not to be swamped by it; to negotiate the rites of baptism and/or confirmation.

But we need discipling throughout our lives, particularly in the areas of relating our faith to work (or unemployment), finances, relationships and stress. Illness, disability, retirement, old age, bereavement, death; these are all times when we need someone to help us.

This chapter opens up a whole new concept in discipling. It is not merely an elementary course in how to become a Christian but an ongoing option for all Christians at all stages of their lives. Ideally we should be able to 'book in' for a period of discipling whenever we are going through a patch of difficulty, a new stage of life (teenage, parenthood, unemployment, retirement etc.) or, like a car that has done a few thousand miles, we feel the need of a 'service'. Christians often do help one another in this way of course, but might it not be a valuable resource to have an established network of discipling available?

4

The 'Who?' of discipling

chapter ten

Who are the disciples?
All Christians, always

Jesus' command to go and make disciples has no limitations other than his return at the end of the age. It is for all time and for all Christians. We never cease to be disciples, we never take the 'L' plates off. There are no days off or holidays. It is a lifestyle, not a job or hobby. Someone who is married is always married; similarly, once a disciple, always a disciple! To be a disciple is to be in a permanent relationship with Jesus Christ.

The whole of our life is meant to be a learning experience: the informal incidents as well as the formal education; the negative disappointments as well as the positive enjoyments; the non-Christian input as well as the Christian teaching; the unexpected contribution as well as the expected advice; the passing moment as well as the extended period.

The disciple must 'fight the good fight, finish the race, and keep the faith' (2 Timothy 4:7); he must be 'faithful, even to the point of death' and so receive 'the crown of life' (Revelation 2:10). There is no retirement, only the final release when God welcomes us home as good and faithful servants.

Newer and weaker Christians

Neither is discipling just for those who feel that they need it, either because they are young in the Christian faith or because they have special needs. There are particular phases of our Christian lives when we have an increased need for discipling, but in differing ways, according to our circumstances, we all need to be disciples all the time. The new Christian can be both a giver as well as a receiver of discipling, for there are many things which older Christians desperately need to hear from younger ones.

Those who feel weak must see themselves as able not only to receive, because in their weakness they have much to offer those who feel they are strong. God uses the weak to shame the strong (1 Corinthians 1:27), and his power is made perfect in weakness; so that when we are weak, then we are strong (2 Corinthians 12:9–10). The picture of the church as a body, and each of us as a part within it, includes the reminder that 'those parts of the body that seem to be weaker are indispensable' (1 Corinthians 12:22). Jesus teaches us that his Kingdom is an upside-down Kingdom in which those who are last will be first, and those who are first will be last (Luke 13:30). So we must never despise the new or the weak or fail to accept their contribution to the discipling process.

Older and stronger Christians

While the mature and able have a responsibility to be discipling others, this must never be to the exclusion of continuing to receive discipling themselves. The warning that if we think we are standing firm we should be careful that we don't fall (1 Corinthians 10:12) is a vital one for all disciplers. One of the greatest dangers for Christian leaders is a lack of accountability. Every 'King David' needs a 'Nathan' to say to him, 'You are the man!' (2 Samuel 12:7). Every older and stronger Christian needs to be opposed to their face when they are clearly wrong, as Paul did to Peter (Galatians 2:11). It is a responsibility and a privilege to bring back one who has wandered from the truth (James 5:19). The Bible is full of examples of those who failed, despite seeming to be strong. Moses, at the height of his leadership, failed to trust God (Numbers 20:12). David, at the height of his kingship, failed by committing adultery and murder (2 Samuel 11). Peter, after spending so much time with Jesus, and after his great boasting, disowned Jesus three times (Matthew 26:31–35, 69–75; Mark 14:27–31, 66–72; Luke 22:31–34, 54–62; John 18:15–18, 25–27). Age and strength bring particular temptations which can only be overcome by a willingness to continue to be a disciple.

Wanting to learn

At the departure of the Pilgrim Fathers on the *Mayflower* in 1620 John Robinson said, 'The Lord has yet more light and truth to break forth from his word.' That should be the motto of every disciple. We are never too old to learn, and if we have the desire, old dogs can always be taught new tricks! It has been a common Christian experience that the more we get to know about God, the more we realize how much we don't yet know. The early desire of the Christian life to know more and more about Christ has to be actively maintained in later life. It is to those who hunger and thirst after righteousness that the blessing of being filled is promised (Matthew 5:6). Learning will not just happen; it will only be achieved when we have a desire for it which is translated into action which makes it happen. How many books lie started but not finished? How many courses are begun but not completed? How many resolutions are made but not carried out? We all make time for what we consider to be of the most importance, and the attitude of the true disciple is to carve out the time which is needed for learning. Even Jesus had to create a time and a place to learn from the Father; very early in the morning (Mark 1:35), or very late at night (Mark 6:46–47), or all night (Luke 6:12), or in lonely places (Luke 5:16).

Open to change

Discipling is not, however, just a question of knowledge, of how much we know; it is even more a matter of application. We can be full of information *about* God and yet never really *know* him. All the doctrine and theology in the world is of no value unless it leads to a life of Christian commitment and obedience. If our learning does not alter our lifestyle, then it is merely academic, like the water that constantly flows into the Dead Sea without flowing out again, ending up lifeless and useless.

Festus accused Paul of being out of his mind because of his great learning, but it was Festus, like Pilate, who knew so much and was so near to faith and yet turned away from the challenge to change (Acts 26:24–29; John 18:28–40). It is possible to handle holy things and yet not be holy ourselves; it is even possible to disciple another and not be changed ourselves. Like Paul, we must always be on our guard that, having preached to others, we ourselves are not disqualified (1 Corinthians 9:27). The disciple's prayer should be 'Lord, change me', rather than 'Lord, change them or it.' Jesus' definition of disciples was 'everyone who hears these words of mine and puts them into practice' (Matthew 7:24), 'who hear the word of God and obey it' (Luke 11:28).

The cost of being a disciple

Being a disciple is costly. It involves curtailing our freedom and accepting the authority of someone else. Their standards and outlook may not be the same as ours. We may not even want to share parts of our lives with them. At times another's discipling may seem like an intrusion. But discipling cannot happen on a take-it-or-leave-it basis: we must trust the discipler, we must be committed to them and we must accept their rights and authority in our lives.

Jesus' disciples often tried to fight a losing battle with him, trying to keep control themselves when they were supposed to be under his authority. Peter wanted to tell Jesus what to do (Mark 8:31–33), to hold on to experiences of God (Mark 9:5–6) and to manage the lives of others (John 21:20–23). Thomas wanted to see some results (John 11:16), to understand things logically (John 14:5) and to have proof (John 20:25). James and John wanted to judge others (Luke 9:54) and to be the top dogs (Mark 10:37). Andrew and Philip wanted to calculate the cost of doing God's will (John 6:5–9). Nathanael wanted to know who Jesus was, to assess his credentials (John 1:45–46). Judas wanted to manage the money (John 13:29; Matthew 26:14–16).

Being a disciple means handing the power over to Christ and to those whom Christ appoints over us. It means submitting 'to one another out of reverence for Christ' (Ephesians 5:21).

Diligence

Being a disciple is hard work. Nothing that is worth achieving comes easily, and Christian growth is the result of many growing pains. Paul's illustrations of the soldier, the athlete and the farmer in 2 Timothy 2 include the ideas of enduring hardship, competition and hard work. Sacrificing other things in order to achieve a result is a high ideal which is so rarely put in to practice by Christians. The prospective disciples who came rushing to Jesus were stopped in their tracks by his apparently negative response: he asked them first to count the cost of losing their home, father, family and money (Luke 9:57–62; 18:18–30). Jesus told them that being a disciple involved a life-long commitment (Luke 9:62) with hard work, no pay, constant opposition (Luke 9:1–6; 10:1–4) and even death (John 21:19). The call to be a disciple is a call to a life of hard labour, requiring the total effort of one's body, mind and spirit. Like Timothy, the disciple is to 'Be diligent in these matters; give yourself wholly to them, so that everyone may see your progress. Watch your life and doctrine closely. Persevere in them' (1 Timothy 4:15–16).

Discernment

The disciple must exercise perception and judgment. Paul's instruction, 'Test everything. Hold on to the good' (1 Thessalonians 5:21) must be applied to all that we receive in discipling. We must know how to distinguish right from wrong; and then there is the much more difficult task of distinguishing the best from the good. So often we accept second best because we are not willing to take the time and effort to search for God's first best. So many short-cuts become cul-de-sacs, so many easy options turn out to be hard knocks, and so many cheap promises are found to be empty. The disciple must be as shrewd as a snake and as innocent as a dove (Matthew 10:16).

Paul prayed for the disciples at Philippi that they would discern what was best (Philippians 1:9–11), and we need to pray that same prayer for ourselves and for others. Lot's lack of discernment in choosing what appeared to be the best land led to disastrous results when the true nature of that land was revealed (Genesis 13:10). Like Christ, we are not to judge by what we see with our eyes or decide by what we hear with our ears; instead we are to 'judge with righteousness' (Isaiah 11:4). True discernment takes time and effort. We must not be satisfied with half-truths, rumour or hearsay; we must seek the truth, the whole truth, and nothing but the truth, so help us God.

Discipline

The word 'disciple' and the word 'discipline' have the same root meaning, which is 'to learn'. The disciple is essentially someone who is involved in a learning process. He or she must submit to the process in order to benefit from its outcome. Someone who is learning to play a musical instrument must reproduce the discipline of the weekly lesson in the discipline of his or her daily practice session, before the exam can be passed or the recital given. A similar principle applies to discipline in the discipling process.

Hebrews 12:1–13 draws important truths about discipline from the example of Jesus (verses 1–3), the love of the Father (verses 4–11), and our responsibility (verses 12–13). Discipline comes from God as a judgment so that we are not condemned (1 Corinthians 11:32). But it should also come from within ourselves, so that we are self-disciplined (Titus 1:8). When the Bible speaks of 'self-discipline' (2 Timothy 1:7) or 'self-control' (Galatians 5:23; 2 Peter 1:6), it is not referring to some kind of self-centred self-help by which we pull ourselves up by our own bootlaces. Christian self-discipline is our response to the Spirit's power and love producing his fruit in us. Only the person who is disciplined by God in their inner being can apply self-discipline to the life which comes from that inner self. Discipline must begin in the heart and mind, for it is from there that all else flows. When God's Spirit controls our spirit, then we can be truly disciplined at our core, and a disciplined life can follow.

chapter eleven

Who are the disciplers?

The discipler's qualities

While Christlikeness is the overall quality needed in a discipler, there are a number of aspects to this which need to be highlighted.

1. The discipler must have a clear conscience
(1 Peter 3:15–16)

For the sake of the one being discipled and the whole church and the wider community, each discipler must be pure and holy before God. Enormous damage is done to a disciple's faith and to the church's reputation when a discipler is discovered to be living a seriously inconsistent life. A clear conscience is far more than not being found out; it is not even harbouring the appearance of evil. This does not mean that only those who are perfect can disciple, otherwise there could be no disciplers at all! Rather, it means that the past has been forgiven and the present is under the authority of Christ. In discipling there is no room for hypocrisy, where what we say with our lips is not true of our lives.

2. The discipler must be prepared to listen

(James 1:19)

A willingness to listen is vital, for in the discipling relationship we must first accept and understand, and only then respond and teach. James says we are to be quick to listen, giving the invitation for another to share, making them feel that they are important and that what they say is worth hearing. He goes on to say that we must be slow to speak and slow to become angry. This does not mean that we cannot talk or react; it means that what we say and do should be a considered and measured response. Thoughts we may keep to ourselves, but the spoken word can never be taken back. Listening not only takes willingness but also preparation. We need to be equipped to listen by ensuring that our bodies, minds and spirits are fit.

3. The discipler must be a burden-bearer

(Galatians 6:1–6)

We cannot remain aloof in the discipling relationship. We must be prepared to get our hands dirty and our backs bent. A discipler who is unwilling to carry another's pack is a contradiction in terms. However, Paul also says that as well as carrying each other's burdens, we are each to carry our own load (verses 2, 5). There must be a progression from total dependence to interdependence. Also there must be a mutual carrying of loads between the discipler and the disciple, for the one who receives instruction must also share with the instructor (verse 6). Discipling will sometimes be hard and costly, but if we are not willing for this, then we should never start. Disciplers must always remain disciples who deny themselves, take up their cross daily, and follow after Christ (Luke 9:23).

4. The discipler must be willing to show love and acceptance (Galatians 5:13)

It is said of Jesus that he accepts us just as we are but loves us too much to leave us like that. A discipler should have a similar attitude. There must be a willingness to receive a person, even when that is misconstrued by others, and to give genuine care and concern, even when that is costly. We must not judge by appearances or categorize by reputation, but through an accepting love we must try to understand fully. First impressions are important, and what we communicate in any way on the first occasion has a lasting effect. If we hesitate or seem horrified, it will be hard for the disciple to forget this. We need the grace of God to guard our reactions and direct our actions.

5. The discipler must be someone with empathetic understanding (2 Corinthians 1:3–7)

The God of all comfort comforts us so that we can comfort others with the comfort which we have received. Empathy goes beyond sympathy. Sympathy is compassion alongside, while empathy is compassion inside – getting inside another person's skin, feeling as they feel and thinking as they think. There is a limit as to how far we can empathize, for we can never fully be another person, but disciplers must follow this pathway as far as they possibly can; they must allow God to give them depths of understanding which naturally they could not have. The disciple needs to feel that the discipler really understands and really cares.

6. The discipler must be consistent and persistent (Colossians 1:28–29)

Discipling is not a short-term, hit-and-run process. Very rarely will we deal with someone's needs overnight. Paul described it as labouring and struggling, as the toil of the worker and the exertion of the athlete, requiring all his energy and power. We must not short-change our disciples by giving them only a half-hearted and limited-term commitment. There needs to be a determination to see the task through. Sir Winston Churchill's words, 'I have nothing to offer but blood, toil, tears and sweat', could well be applied to the discipler, except that there is something else to offer – the deep joy and satisfaction of 'presenting everyone perfect in Christ'.

Paul's qualifications for overseers (1 Timothy 3:2–7) provide a good checklist for disciplers. It can be summarized as the three Ms – maturity, meekness and mastery. Disciplers need maturity of character and understanding, so that they are at least one step ahead of the disciple, to offer a goal and an aim, and an example to be followed. Disciplers also need meekness of spirit, an admission that they do not know it all, and are willing to receive as well as to give. Finally, disciplers need to have mastery of their own selves and lives, so that they can help to manage others and their lives. Disciplers – those who wish to disciple others – must first be discipled themselves. A teachable spirit is one of the most needed qualities.

The fruit of the Spirit – 'love, joy, peace, kindness, goodness, faithfulness, gentleness, and self-control' (Galatians 5:22–3) – is the best summary of the type of characteristics disciplers should have.

The discipler's abilities

While the personal qualities which disciplers need are the *fruit* of the Spirit, the abilities which they need to carry out a discipling ministry are the *gifts* of the Spirit. The New Testament gives us the following lists of gifts:

1 Corinthians 12:8–11. The message of wisdom, the message of knowledge, faith, gifts of healing, miraculous powers, prophecy, distinguishing between spirits, speaking in tongues, and the interpretation of tongues
1 Corinthians 12:28–30. Apostles, prophets, teachers, workers of miracles, healers, helpers, administrators, speakers in tongues and interpreters
Romans 12:6–8. Prophesying, serving, teaching, encouraging, contributing leadership and showing mercy
Ephesians 4:11–12. Apostles, prophets, evangelists, pastors and teachers
1 Peter 4:10–11. Speaking and serving.

All these gifts are tools in the toolbox of the discipler, to be used as the need arises though no-one will expect to receive them all. Some gifts will become a more permanent ability, while others will be an occasional ability given for a specific purpose or situation. These gifts must all be exercised under the authority of Christ and his church. All must be used with love, the greatest gift of all.

The discipler's training

In order to develop his or her personality and ability, a discipler must always be undergoing training. Systematic study of Scripture and a consistent prayer life are needed both for the discipler's own spiritual growth and for that of the disciple. Regular worship and fellowship are essential for the discipler to receive from God and from others, and for the disciple to become fully integrated into the family of the church. Studying relevant books and tapes and taking appropriate courses should be part of the ongoing training.

The discipler's experience

Ultimately only practice makes perfect, and while we must not experiment with disciples, there comes a point at which the discipler must begin to disciple. This may need to be done alongside another discipler to begin with. The discipler should always be supported by supervision. When all is said and done, experience is the most important qualification.

The discipler's resources

The discipler's first resource is his or her own self. Who we are, what we have received, where we have been, when we have lived, how we have seen things, and why we are as we are – all these things go to make up our personal resources. Our personality, experience and education blend together to be the 'me' which is offered to the disciple. The *only* thing we have to offer anyone is ourselves, but that is the greatest gift that we can give. So many people are fobbed off with material gifts when what they really want is a little of someone's time and attention. It is costly to give my real self rather than the person I wish I were or others think I am, and it's risky for them to accept the real me rather than the person they would like to receive or others think they need.

Another important resource for the discipler is his or her family. The discipler who is married and is a parent is either an advantage which needs to be capitalized on or a disadvantage which needs to be compensated for in each particular situation. We must not get locked into a strait-jacket which only allows us to disciple those who are like us in every respect. In discipling we must allow both our differences and our similarities to contribute to the process. Our family will be a resource for us by their influence and support; and they may be a direct resource for the disciple, although this needs to be carefully considered and must have the agreement of both the disciple and the family. We must allow family members to exercise their own ministry from their own gifting and not assume that they will necessarily be involved in discipling just because we are.

Next, the discipler's friends are a resource for both. They can give the discipler their prayers, wisdom, encouragement and practical support. For the disciple they can be a nurturing social group, and he or she can benefit from their experience and expertise. The book of Proverbs reminds us that while a friend should love at all times (Proverbs 17:17), it is also the wounds from a friend that can be trusted (27:6). But gossip separates close friends (16:28). There are certain things we may need to hear which can only be said to us by a friend, things we would not accept from anyone else. Friendship must be cultivated with caution (12:26) and not forsaken by neglect (27:10). In John 15:13–15 Jesus reminded his disciples of the cost of friendship ('we lay down our life for our friends'), the definition of friendship ('you are my friends if you do what I command') and the essence of friendship ('I no longer call you servants. . . Instead, I have called you friends').

The Christian fellowship to which the discipler belongs is another important resource. The church provides an equipping, empowering and encouraging environment. It is the place where a discipler can receive scriptural teaching, prayer support and practical help. The discipler should not try to go it alone as a one-man band. In discipling he or she will hear things from the disciple which are confidential, but while the discipler cannot discuss these things with a third party, they should never fail to share themselves. As the church recognizes and appoints disciplers, so there must be a strong, on-going support system for them throughout the discipling process. Both the church and the discipler have a responsibility to be mutually accountable and accessible.

Next, the discipler should have access to some professional resources. While discipling is not a profession, there are some professional skills which the discipler can usefully learn. The many others who are regularly involved in discipling work are also a potential resource for the discipler. Discipling needs to have a professional approach so that what we do is the best it can possibly be. The discipler should be aware of the many resources available from various Christian organizations (see *Resources*), and churches should ensure that a resource centre for disciplers as well as disciples is set up. These resources should not be exclusively Christian, but should also draw from experts in the secular field who have interpersonal and educational skills.

Supervision of the discipler

The discipler's prime supervisor is God, who speaks through his Word and his Spirit to our conscience and spirit. We should also be supervised by other people, both friends and professionals. Thirdly, there is self-supervision or self-assessment, in which we monitor our own behaviour and correct it if necessary. There should never be 'Lone Ranger disciplers', going off and doing their own thing. Every discipler should be accountable to someone else, not just in theory but in reality and practice.

Support for the discipler

The discipler needs constant support. Knowing that there are others who will share with us the discipling tasks which we accept is essential and encouraging. These supporters should include parents, partner, family, friends, leaders and other disciplers. We are never alone and the Holy Spirit, who is the Counsellor who comes alongside us, ministers his presence through the people whom he places with us. Paul often spoke of his fellow workers and partners with great joy; he also felt deep sadness when no-one supported him and everyone deserted him (2 Timothy 4:16).

Part four in a nutshell

Who are the disciples? Simply all Christians, the newer and weaker, the older and stronger . . . all who are willing to learn, who are open to change and who are willing to face the cost of change, in a word all those who are able to embrace *discipline*.

The disciplers must also be committed Christians but we are not looking for qualified professionals. The 'qualifications' needed are a good conscience (not 'sinless perfection'!), patience to listen, bear burdens and to accept and love; evidence of the fruit of the Spirit. Perhaps the majority of ordinary Christians can be and should be disciplers. In addition experience, training where available, reading (see p. 157) and use of other resources can be a great help. All disciplers should be *supervised* by others, that is, in a sense, discipled themselves, able to unburden themselves (though not breaking confidences) and receive support from another. The whole enterprise is a team effort. There must be no 'lone ranger' disciplers. We are all accountable, under God, to someone in the church.

So, the extent of those who need to be discipled stretches to the very edges of the church but also those who can be disciplers are around in great abundance. Many will be unwilling to acknowledge such a role (even if they are already acting as disciplers 'unofficially'): some of us will be unprepared to commit ourselves to something new; some may be genuinely unfitted for the task – our gifts vary greatly and church leaders need to discern them with prayer and care. The fact remains that few churches can genuinely claim to have no-one who needs help and nobody who could, with assistance, do a little discipling.

5

The 'How?' of discipling

chapter twelve

It takes two to disciple
Listening

Being a good listener is the primary qualification for being a discipler. Proverbs 18:13 tells us that 'He who answers before listening – that is his folly and his shame', and James 1:19 says that 'Everyone should be quick to listen, slow to speak and slow to become angry.'

Good listening is both an attitude of the mind and an expression of the body. It has been summed up in the acronym SOLER, which means 'Squarely face; Open posture; Lean forward; Eye contact; Relax'. In our listening we should:

Be accepting of people just as they are, warts and all, including their difficulties and feelings. If a person senses that we do not really want to hear what they have to say, then they will not be willing to risk sharing with us.

Be concerned about people, showing that concern through involvement and relationship, and empathizing with all that they face. We are not to be mere recording machines which just absorb information with no response; we are to be fellow human beings who feel and react.

Be patient by showing an unhurried, quiet and tolerant attitude, even when conflicts arise. Our motto should be 'Please be patient – God hasn't finished with me yet!' It's not always easy for someone to tell us about themselves, and so we must give them time to do so. We must also resist the temptation to put words into people's mouths or to finish their sentences for them, however irritating it is for us to have to wait for the obvious.

Be attentive by showing interest in the person and demonstrating our commitment to listen. We must not jump to our own conclusions, nor make superficial comparisons with others, nor assume from initial information that we understand the whole situation.

Listening to all that is said is vital if there is to be real discipling. We must be able to receive all the input that is being given to us. We must listen to:

The words that are said and how they are said. There can be a world of difference in meaning between the same word said in two completely different ways. For example, 'I am coping' may mean that I am doing fine, or it may mean that I am barely surviving.

The silences that occur and when and why they come. Silences need to be interpreted. Is the person hesitating because of fear? Or groping for the right words? Or struggling to say something which is very difficult for them to admit? Or is it merely a natural pause in the conversation? Do not always rush in to break a silence. Silences can be healing.

The thinking that is going on. We need to sense or ask what the disciple's thoughts are. Sometimes a whole cascade of thought only needs a simple encouragement to be vocalized. People need time to think, but that thought should not be lost by a failure to create an opportunity for it to be expressed.

The emotions and feelings that lie behind the outward vocal and visible expressions. The way in which a particular key word is said or avoided may be the way in to a whole area of new and important conversation. We need to be especially aware of words which are said without the expected feelings, such as 'love' or 'hate' being said with no accompanying expression of warmth or anger.

The facial expressions which may reinforce or contradict what is being said. A person may say 'Yes' when their face is saying 'No', and vice versa. A person may say that there is nothing wrong, when tears or a frown may indicate that things are far from well.

The body language, such as posture, position, tension, movement, coughing or stuttering. All this can give important clues as to what is happening in the person's heart, mind and spirit. It is important, however, not to read too much into body language. We need to take time before being able to place a person on a scale of response from 'extrovert' to 'introvert'. We should not assume a lack of feeling just because a person is very 'laid back', but if such a person suddenly becomes very expressive in their body language, we should be asking ourselves why.

Levels of communication will vary within discipling, but there should be an attempt to move communication on through the levels. These levels have been defined as:
Cliché conversation, which centres around generalizations and keeps the parties at arm's length.
Narrative, which confines the conversation to facts and information.

Sharing ideas, in which opinions and beliefs become part of the conversation.

Sharing feelings, which allows emotions to be expressed.

Open and honest communication, in which there are no boundaries to what can be voiced.

For example, a conversation may start with the weather (cliché), then move on to the person's work (narrative), then to discussing certain types of work (sharing ideas), then to the person expressing frustration with their job (sharing feelings), and finally to a discussion of whether the person should resign from the position (open and honest communication).

Responding

This is the other side of the coin to listening, and it is done both subconsciously and overtly, non-verbally and verbally.

In non-verbal response, just as we 'listen' to another person's body language, so they are 'listening' to ours. The yawn or the distant stare can negate all our statements that we are interested and concerned. We need to be aware of our own body language as much as that of our disciples. Often we need help in this area, either by allowing someone else to watch us and then comment, or by being videoed and then watching ourselves. Jesus, Peter, John and Paul all looked straight at those they encountered (Luke 22:61; Acts 3:4; 14:9). Jesus placed his hands on, took aside, bent down to, took in his arms, wept with, and even spat on those he met! We must allow our whole being to respond to those whom we disciple: our whole body, and not just our tongues; our whole mind, and not just our verbalized thoughts, our whole spirit, 'with groans that words cannot express' (Romans 8:26).

In verbal response we need to remember that it is not only *what* we say that matters, but also *how* we say it. In general we probably ask too many questions and become inquisitorial, so we should be constantly thinking, 'Why do I need to ask this question?' We should avoid 'Why?' questions, either/or questions and series of questions. Instead we should be asking 'What?', 'When?', 'Where?', 'Who?' and 'How?' questions. If we are asking a question we should do so plainly and not dress it up as a statement. If we are responding with a statement we should make it a direct one and not phrase it as a question.

An old saying tells us that we have 'two ears to listen and one mouth to speak', which suggests that we should listen twice as much as we speak! As the discipler we are the enabler, and so we should not take centre stage, but should be in a supporting role. We should be alongside the disciple to listen and prompt, to understand and reflect, and only then to assess and direct. Jesus challenged those who had ears to use them (Mark 4:23), and he asked his disciples how it was that, having ears, they failed to hear (Mark 8:18). Often we are so busy talking that we fail to really listen, or we fail to hear because we are thinking about something else. If only we always listened before we spoke we would avoid saying a lot of unnecessary and unhelpful words. Those 'who answer before listening – that is their folly and their shame' (Proverbs 18:13).

Assessing

We need to evaluate a conversation both by what is included and what is absent. We must be specific and concrete, challenging abstract responses; objective and dispassionate in our judgment; genuine and honest in our appraisal; and sure in our understanding of the present situation. We must actually determine the level of need. Is the disciple experiencing a problem, or a predicament, or a crisis, or panic, or shock? We must distinguish between symptoms and causes, between what is the presented immediate issue and what is the hidden long-term issue. The following check-list can give us pointers to this:

What is said or not said? Which topics were addressed and which ones were ignored? We particularly need to watch out for misunderstandings or different understandings of a topic, which may be genuine or may be a way of avoiding certain areas. For example, if a person constantly understands 'family' as meaning the church family, we need to find out whether this is simply their terminology or whether they are trying to avoid any reference to their natural family.

Why is something said or not said? We need to respect a person's agenda but not be limited by it. A person may make it very clear that they want to talk about their anger at failing to get a particular job, and, while we must address this, we must not be trapped into failing to look at other dimensions. For example, were they truly motivated to try and get this job in the first place?

When were things said or not said? How did various areas relate together and where did they come in the discussion? This especially applies to the beginning and the end of conversations. Some things may be said almost in passing at the start in order to get them out of the way, in the hope that they will not be raised again. Others may be slipped in at the end, with the idea that they will be passed over without too much attention, or sometimes to try to prolong the session when you have come to the agreed time for ending it.

How were things said or not said? Did the person say that they felt that certain things must be said and others definitely not said? Any spiritual pressure or even blackmail must be challenged, so statements such as 'God has said we should talk about this or not talk about that' need to be treated with care and caution, and the discipler's own spiritual understanding must be added to that claimed by the disciple.

Directing

An important issue in discipling is whether it should be directive or non-directive. The extremes of the manipulative puppeteer who totally controls the disciple and the laid-back spectator who is never involved must be avoided. However, the middle ground between them is very wide, and great skill is needed to navigate it successfully. There is a time to lead and a time to follow, a time to state and a time to suggest, a time to give and a time to withhold. Disciplers must know their disciples well enough to understand how they will react to particular approaches, and to grasp when they need a directive response and when a non-directive one is required.

Another key issue in discipling is whether it should be

judgmental or non-judgmental. It is important to initially suspend judgment. First impressions may have to be drastically revised in the light of later discoveries, and the damage of rash responses is hard to repair. There will often be a place for the expression of loving judgment, the truth spoken in love (Ephesians 4:15), but the right to speak in such a way has to be earned. It is only those who are spiritual who can make judgments about all things – those who have been 'instructed by the Lord' and have 'the mind of Christ' (1 Corinthians 2:15–16).

Yet another important issue in discipling is knowing when to agree with what the disciple is saying and when to challenge it. The discipler's role needs to be fully understood. They are meant to be a catalyst who provokes, a communicator who educates, and a conciliator who resolves. Each of these functions will require a blend of agreeing and challenging, of inviting and guiding. We must be very careful of our motives here, not agreeing just for the sake of peace or simply under pressure; equally, we should not disagree just in order to provoke or primarily to maintain our own standing. There are points at which we have to state the truth as we see it, whatever the cost. However, there is always an appropriate way to say it which makes it easier for the disciple to receive it.

chapter thirteen

Who disciples who?
Male and female

As a rule there should be no one-to-one discipling carried out by members of opposite sexes. However innocent things might seem, we are not only to avoid all immorality but even the hint of it (Ephesians 5:3). The only possible exception to this rule would be in discipling children, when a 'parent' figure of either sex could be the discipler. But in view of the present climate regarding child abuse, even this could need very careful appointment and supervision. However, one type of discipling in which both sexes can safely be involved is where one married couple disciples another couple.

Sadly, it also needs to be said that even in same-sex discipling care and attention must continue to be exercised so that no unwholesome relationships develop, especially homosexual ones.

The church leaders who are directing the discipling must accept that, having made the introductions, they are accountable to keep a check on the situation that develops, for they are meant to keep watch over people 'as those who must give an account' (Hebrews 13:17).

Also the disciplers must heed James' warning that not many should presume to be teachers, because they know that those who teach will be judged more strictly (James 3:1).

Old and young

Differences of age between discipler and disciple have advantages and disadvantages. A similarity of age can help to foster a rapport, but it may also lead to an unhelpful cosiness. An age gap may make it harder for disciple and discipler to relate to each other, but it can also bring a dimension which would otherwise be missing. Paul instructs Timothy about the relationships between older and younger Christians: 'Do not rebuke an older man harshly, but exhort him as if he were your father. Treat younger men as brothers, older women as mothers, and younger women as sisters, with absolute purity' (1 Timothy 5:1-2). Both Peter and John address the same issue (1 Peter 5:5; 1 John 2:12-14). While the age difference between the disciple and the discipler is an important factor, it should not be the determining one. Often the most unlikely age mix can produce the most outstanding results in discipling.

Mature and new

The discipler must possess a degree of maturity which is beyond that of the one being discipled – probably a little more than being just one step ahead! However, it is possible for new Christians with a little experience to disciple others, provided that the disciple also has access to more mature Christians in other areas and the discipler has sufficient assistance.

Due weight must be given to Paul's prohibition of recent converts being overseers (1 Timothy 3:6). We should remember, however, that discipling is not the same thing as leading, and that in a new church like the one at Ephesus, which would have been at most ten years old, a 'recent convert' meant someone who had been a Christian for a matter of months rather than years.

Maturity should not be measured only in terms of length of time, since within just a few months of their conversion some Christians grow in faith far more than some others who were converted many years ago. Maturity should be assessed in relation to personality, natural gifts and abilities, and the work of God's Spirit.

Different personalities

It needs to be recognized that human nature may not be able to cope with the strains of too vast a personality difference between disciple and discipler. The preferences and abilities of both people must be taken into account. The best 'match' in each situation should be the aim, whether this is achieved by similar or dissimilar partners. While the obvious may be a good general rule, it should not be applied to the exclusion of the unexpected. Sometimes the most unlikely people become the best discipler and disciple, rather like

magnets where opposite poles attract each other. Sometimes the personnel options will be rather limited, and
so we may have to accept a pairing which is less than
ideal, since it is better to offer some discipling rather
than none at all.

Good results can follow if both parties are willing
to try to make it work. Paul and many of his
disciples, for example, Barnabas, John Mark, Silas,
Timothy and Titus, had very different personalities,
and yet those relationships worked. Probably the
'bold' Paul and the 'timid' Timothy learned a lot
from each other (see 2 Corinthians 10:1; 2 Timothy
1:7).

'As iron sharpens iron'

This biblical phrase (Proverbs 27:17) speaks about how
people learn from one another. It is better to have a
discipling relationship in which sparks fly than one in
which there is no spark at all! Different personalities can
produce understanding and acceptance, differing view-
points can produce perception and tolerance, and
different outlooks can enrich and extend. However, if
the 'sharpening of iron' is the only thing which is
happening in a particular discipling relationship, then it
must be an unbalanced and unhelpful one. As well as
flying sparks, the disciple also needs the joy of 'perfume
and incense', 'the pleasantness of one's friend' which
'springs from his earnest counsel' (Proverbs 27:9).
Discipling needs to be sharpening but also soothing,
stimulating but also sheltering, stretching but also
supporting.

'Chalk and cheese'

This is not a biblical phrase, and yet it points to the scriptural principle that God has made us all different and we are meant to learn from each other's differences. Disciplers are not meant to make clones of themselves in their discipling, neither should disciples only accept the discipling that fits in with their own personality. There needs to be a stretching development for both through the discipling process. Differences should enrich, not detract, and each should come to the end of the discipling course with a fuller understanding of the other and with new resources to face their own lives and their continuing discipling. Paul wrote, 'If the whole body were an eye, where would the sense of hearing be? If the whole body were an ear, where would the sense of smell be?' (1 Corinthians 12:17). He used this ludicrous picture to make the point that we all need each other, and we need each other to be *different*. Sadly, some disciplers try to turn their disciples into carbon copies of themselves, with disastrous consequences.

The best of friends?

What is the essence of the discipling relationship? Is it to be confined to the task of discipling or does it extend beyond that? There needs to be a balance of friendship and formality. Discipling should not degenerate into mere 'chumminess', neither should it be so rigid as to be devoid of any real companionship. Friendship should be a hallmark of discipling, but the depth of that friendship will vary, and the connection between the level of friendship and the degree of effectiveness is not a direct one. Some aspects of discipling are better carried out by a discipler who is a friend, but not a close friend of the disciple. Conversely, some types of discipling and some individual disciples need a deep level of friendship. Friendship in discipling should always be a help and never a deterrent; when friendship gets in the way of discipling, then that friendship needs looking at very closely. Paul, Peter, John and Jude all addressed their disciples as dear friends in their letters, so present-day disciplers should be able to do the same.

Purely professional?

While the discipler needs to take a professional approach to the task, it is not simply a professional exercise. Boundaries and detachment may have to be established, but never to the degree that they rob the discipling of any warmth. The discipler needs to be well prepared and trained for the task, but he or she should not become so distinct and detached that there is no rapport. The pursuit of excellence and the pathway of accreditation in Christian ministry are good things, so long as they do not rob that ministry of the personal touch. Disciples must never become mere numbers or cyphers. In their accounts of the calling of the twelve disciples by Jesus, the gospels give us a full list of their names (Matthew 10:1–4; Mark 3:13–19; Luke 6:12–16), and the list is repeated at the beginning of the book of Acts (Acts 1:12–14). Disciplers, like the Good Shepherd, should know and call their sheep by name (John 10:3, 14).

Spiritual or social?

Discipling involves growth in body, mind and spirit, so all these must feature in the process. The body is to be 'the temple of the Holy Spirit' (1 Corinthians 6:19), the mind is to be 'the mind of Christ' (1 Corinthians 2:16), and the spirit is to be 'one with the Lord' (1 Corinthians 6:17). Paul prayed that the Thessalonians' whole spirit, soul and body would be sanctified and kept blameless by God (1 Thessalonians 5:23), and that needs to be the prayer and goal of every disciple and discipler. Since learning happens by both hearing and seeing, the discipler must be willing both to teach and to show Christian maturity in body, mind and spirit. Interaction at a variety of levels and in a number of ways is vital, and social contact should supplement spiritual truth. The disciple would be able to see Christlikeness in every part of the discipler's life, and so be urged to imitate them (1 Corinthians 4:16).

Dealing with differences

Every relationship faces problems, and discipling is no exception. Yet the very resolving of such problems is an important part of the discipling process. Differences will be real and deep, but the ability to face them honestly and come to terms with them will teach lessons which may well not be learned in any other way. It is important to distinguish between problems which arise from the content of the discipling course and those which come from the personalities involved. In particular, the discipler will have to be aware that as they deal with painful issues there is a temptation for the disciple to vent their frustration or anger on the discipler. This reflection will need to be accepted at first, but at the opportune time it should be raised and dealt with. Where there are interpersonal conflicts, these will need to be resolved in a biblical way, particularly in accordance with Matthew 18:15–17.

Who has the casting vote?

The old saying that it is possible to win the argument but lose the person is never more true than in discipling. This is not a battle to be fought but a person to be helped. Progress will only be made by consensus, not by forcing issues through. What is at stake is not the reputation of the discipler but the growth of the disciple. Issues must neither be blown up out of all proportion nor so minimized that they are left to fester through neglect. The discipler has a particular responsibility to take the first step and to make the first move in resolving matters. The book of Proverbs is full of wise advice in this regard. For example, it says, 'A gentle answer turns away wrath, but a harsh word stirs up anger' (Proverbs 15:1).

When to change?

When things are really not working out, it is much better to acknowledge this and make changes than to soldier on regardless. It is a sign of maturity for a discipler appropriately to hand over a disciple to someone else when unable to carry out the discipling. When things do need to be changed it is best to avoid apportioning blame, but simply to part on good terms. The first discipler should resist the temptation to prime the next discipler on what they see as the faults and failings of the disciple. Certain helpful information should be passed on, but unhelpful things should be left unsaid. Nothing should be said privately which they would not be prepared to say in the presence of the disciple. Where a disciple or discipler often changes partners due to not being able to get on, this should be looked at with a view to discovering any underlying reasons, which could then be dealt with. The example of Paul and John Mark shows us that blessing and reconciliation can eventually come out of discord and disharmony (compare Acts 15:37–38 and 2 Timothy 4:11). Paul's letter to Philemon about Onesimus is an illustration of how correctly to handle issues that one person may create between two others.

chapter fourteen

Beginnings and endings
The pairing of disciple and discipler

This has so many ramifications that it must involve a third party. The church leaders cannot abdicate their responsibilities here, for both the value of the disciple and the importance of the discipling demand extensive prayer and care in making the right decisions. Mistakes made here cannot easily be rectified later. Subjective sensitivity must be mixed with objective reality. The disciple must have confidence in the discipler who is allocated to them, especially if the person is as yet not known to them; and this confidence can come only through their trust in those who are appointing the discipler. The discipler, too, needs to feel that the person they are to disciple is the right one for them, and that they can have such certainty because of their faith in those who are making the choices.

Church leaders' decisions here cannot be authoritarian, and there must be room for discussion with those involved. The aim is to make the best possible pairing, and all those involved must both accept and be happy with the answer which is reached. The question of whether one particular discipler can be involved in a number of one-to-one discipling relationships does not have a simple answer, as it depends on their ability and availability. Nevertheless, the temptation to overload a person who is a good discipler must be resisted.

Agendas and parameters

The current vogue for 'citizens' charters' challenges the church to ensure that it delivers what it promises. Disciples must know what they are being offered, and disciplers must be clear about their responsibilities. This cannot be left to chance but must be carefully thought through and openly expressed, even if it is not formally written down. Content needs to be defined and boundaries drawn. It is better to start small and to increase than offer too much at the beginning and later have to rescind it. Openly admitting at the beginning the limitations involved is more honest and acceptable than implying that there are none and subsequently causing disappointment and disillusionment. These responsibilities rest not only with the church and the discipler, but also with the disciple, who should make his or her own position quite plain.

Special care is needed in setting the agenda when this is not already established either in a church discipling course or by some other means, and sometimes a third party will be needed in order to achieve a mutually acceptable outcome. Setting parameters brings a security of boundaries for both disciple and discipler, and again, these may need to be established and maintained by another person. There can only be a counting of the cost of the discipling process if the information to do so is available to both disciple and discipler.

The first meeting

The first meeting of the disciple and the discipler is crucial and should always be seen more in terms of starting a relationship than of giving information. The quality of the foundations built here will determine the future worth of the discipling course. Careful thought should be given to place and time as well as to approach and content. There are advantages and disadvantages to the meeting being held on either the disciple's or the discipler's home ground, and a neutral venue may not solve any difficulties. The prime concern is to create an environment which helps rather than hinders. The choice of place for the first meeting need not determine where the following ones are held. The presence of a third party may be helpful on this occasion, especially when they have been involved in some way in setting up the discipling relationship. Sufficient time should be allowed both to make introductions and to make some progress, but the meeting should not be so long that it makes the disciple feel uneasy. The time-span agreed beforehand should be kept, unless there are very clear reasons for extending it. It is as important for the disciple to get to know the discipler as the other way round, and there should be plenty of time for this to happen. Beyond this, it is helpful to sketch out the proposed route of the discipling course and the anticipated progress.

Either party should be free to withdraw at this stage without it causing any problems.

How often should you meet?

It is better to offer less and achieve it than to offer more and not achieve it. It is easier to increase the frequency of the meetings than to decrease it. Both parties must be realistic about what they can accept, bearing in mind the preparation and follow-up associated with each occasion. People generally over-estimate their capabilities in this respect, and over-enthusiasm and unattainable goals must be avoided.

If there are marked changes in the frequency of the meetings, the real reason for this needs to be known so that action can be taken. Things should not be allowed to gradually slide away or slowly fade out. If circumstances dictate that the meetings are infrequent, then some form of contact in between sessions, such as a phone call or a brief chat at church, should be considered. There is a value in arranging a regular time each week so that the discipling becomes a fixed priority in the diaries of the participants, although such an arrangement should not become inflexible. The cancellation of appointments should be discouraged, so as to emphasize the importance of commitment by both parties. If the continuation of the discipling course is dependent on the completion of some kind of 'homework' task and this has not been done, the meeting should deal only with the reasons for this and should not move on regardless, even if this means an unusually short meeting.

The format of the meetings

Each meeting must include both review and progression, looking back and looking forward. In addition, there may need to be a major review at key points in the course. Learning must be consolidated and goals must be checked. The discipler must make sure that the achievement to date is secure and can be the basis for future development. Topics need to be explored, understood and acted upon. They need to be explored in the knowledge and experience of both the disciple and the discipler, understood from both an objective and a subjective viewpoint, and acted upon with resolve and realism.

Tasks must be mutually agreed and the continuation of the course should be dependent on their completion. Like homework, they should be noted in a diary and done by the date agreed. However, timetables must be a servant to help progress, not a master which demands completion at any cost. It will be unhelpful if the disciple thinks he or she *must* finish the homework, irrespective of quality or quantity, let alone understanding. Coming to know the landscape is more important than the amount of ground covered.

How the discipling course progresses within the chosen format depends upon the needs of the disciple in question. Is the relationship one between teacher and pupil, master and apprentice, lecturer and student, trainer and trainee, leader and follower, or guide and learner? Whatever method of discipling is appropriate and whichever format is chosen, these need to be the *means* of achieving the *end* of growth, never the end in themselves.

Ending the course

The end of a discipling course will be accompanied by some feeling of bereavement. Both the disciple and the discipler may feel some anger that the course is coming to an end or that expectations have not been fulfilled. Or they may feel grief that things will not continue to be the same and that a relationship is being taken away. Or they may feel guilty that they have ended the course, or that it is their fault that it is not continuing. Or they may feel relief that it is all over and they will not have to meet again. Or they may feel pleasure, knowing that good things have been accomplished.

Any of these feelings may be present, and they need to be acknowledged and expressed so that both parties can continue their Christian lives in a healthy way. Anger must be traced to its source and dealt with appropriately through communication and forgiveness. Grief needs to be seen as real and time must be given for the grieving process to begin to take place. Guilt must be linked to its cause. If it is false guilt, it must be exposed and dispersed, but if it is genuine guilt, then it must be resolved through confession and forgiveness. Relief must be owned up to, and should be seen as either a natural 'end-of-term' response or as an interpersonal issue that needs to be dealt with before either disciple or discipler can move on. Discipling is not an end in itself but a means to the next stage, and the ending of a course can offer a good opportunity for growth if it is handled correctly for and by each person.

Referral to another discipler, either for further discipling or because the present one cannot continue, must be approached carefully and with regard to what is best for the disciple. A clear handing over must happen, which should include some kind of overlap between the two disciplers. All the issues raised above in connection with the ending of the course need to be considered and dealt with here also. If the referring is in order to receive more specialist help, it may be appropriate for the original discipler to continue involvement alongside the new one, if that is acceptable to both the disciple and the new discipler. No sense of confusion or competition must be allowed to develop, however. Referral should never be seen by either the disciple or the discipler as indicating some kind of deficiency or failure on their part, but as a positive step forward in the discipling process. Great care should be taken as to who the disciple is referred to, and all the criteria regarding the first appointment should be followed again. Referral to specialist help should be done with the full knowledge and agreement of the disciple who should never be made to feel that he or she is being passed on from pillar to post like some kind of unwanted article.

Moving from one-to-one discipling to group discipling is a much harder transition, and it demands sensitivity and contact between the discipler and the group leader. The difficulties of this move should not discourage the disciple from attempting it, and the final outcome of one-to-one discipling should always be integration into a larger group. This will eventually involve the full co-operation of all those concerned – not only the disciple, the discipler and the group leader, but also the other members of the group, who will perhaps be the major key to the successful integration of the disciple into their group.

Sadly, this is a point of particular vulnerability and

loss, especially for new Christians. So many of them who are discipled on a one-to-one basis never arrive in a nurture group or a church housegroup. For more mature disciples, one-to-one discipling needs to be carried out alongside an existing or new group. This raises the issue of the relationship between the discipler and the group leader. This should be as open as possible, within the boundaries of confidentiality and respect for the disciple concerned, and it should be with their knowledge and agreement. The discipling process should be working towards integration not just in a small group, but also in the larger group of the whole church. This is not easy because there is something in the closeness and comfort of one-to-one discipling which militates against other relationships.

The beginning of a friendship?

All endings have the potential to be new beginnings, and the completion of a discipling course should mark the start of a new phase in a continuing and yet changed relationship. When discipler and disciple cease to be in that particular association, there needs to be a conscious step and genuine effort to establish and develop a new one. An ended discipling relationship will probably not, of its own accord, become a deep friendship, but, like any other friendship, it will have to be deliberately worked at, hard and long.

It should not be assumed that just because a discipling relationship has existed, it must translate itself into a deep friendship. Many other factors will be present here, including the personalities involved and the possibilities and practicalities for each person. This may be especially true for the disciplers, who will see their priority as discipling, and may not be able to give themselves to on-going deep friendships with each person they disciple. Where the relationship after discipling does not continue at the same level or develop in the way expected, this needs to be carefully discussed so that any potential disappointment or hurt is minimized. The discipler's final responsibility is not the last meeting of the course, but the act of successfully moving the disciple on to the next phase of their Christian life, whatever that may be.

Part five in a nutshell

Discipling skills are closely allied to listening skills – a good listener will probably make a good discipler. The basics of good listening are given in this chapter. In addition to listening a discipler needs sometimes to *direct*, to give information and advice. This needs to be done sensitively and with great care.

A practical question concerns the choice of partner-ship. Leaders need wisdom in knowing whom to put together. Sometimes old and young will go well and opposites may 'gel', but male/female pairings are at best not helpful and at worst disastrous. The relationship may become a friendship, but it needs both to be sharpened as well as smoothed.

Finally the nuts and bolts of how to begin, drawing up agendas, how to organize the course, when and how to end it. Prior agreement is essential to avoid hurt and even 'bereavement'.

From the foregoing it is clear that there are biblical

and common-sense grounds for embarking on a one-to-one discipling scheme; that it will be of value at all times in our Christian lives, especially times of crisis and that very many of us could benefit by helping and being helped. No edifice of organization need be erected and no professional qualifications are needed, though careful supervision is essential. So where do we go from here? A list of further books on this topic, a list of discipling courses in book form and organizations publishing discipleship courses will be found in *Resources* opposite.

Resources

While most of the books listed below are designed for group work, they are equally suitable for one-to-one discipling.

Books about discipling

Anton Baumohl, *Making Adult Disciples: Learning and Teaching in the Local Church* (Scripture Union, 1984).

Alice Fryling, *Disciplemakers' Handbook* (IVP, 1989).

Nicky Gumbel, *Telling others* (Kingsway, 1994).

Billie Hanks and William Shell, *Discipleship* (Word, 1981, 1993).

Bill Hull, *Jesus Christ, Disciple Maker* (Crossway, 1984).

Juan Ortiz, *A Call to Discipleship* (Bridge, 1975).

Juan Ortiz, *Disciple* (Marshalls, 1975).

Anne Ortlund, *Discipling One Another: Discipline for Christian Community* (Word, 1979).

David Watson, *Discipleship* (Hodder, 1981).

John Young, *Discipleship* (Scripture Union, 1989).

Discipling courses in book form

John Allan, *Just Looking* (Bible Society, 1994).

Stephen Gaukroger, *Making it Work* (Scripture Union, 1990).

Stephen Gaukroger, *Being Baptized* (Marshall Pickering, 1993).

John Stott, *Your Confirmation: A Christian Handbook for Adults* (Hodder, 1991).

Arthur Wallis, *Living God's Way: A Course for discipling new Christians* (Kingsway, 1984).

Arthur Wallis, *Going on God's Way* (Kingsway, 1984).

Organizations publishing discipleship courses

While most of the series listed below are designed for group work, they are equally suitable for one-to-one situations.

BIBLE SOCIETY, Stonehill Green, Westlea, Swindon, Wiltshire SN5 7DG
    Building on experience
    Jigsaw
    Modern Christian Living for Women
    New Life
    Old Testament Characters

CRUSADE FOR WORLD REVIVAL, Waverley Abbey House, Waverley Lane, Farnham, Surrey GU9 8EP
    Every Day with Jesus Exploring the Bible
    Every Day with Jesus for Growing Christians